# Tracie and Jody

A Lasting Lesbian Love Story

1

**ANITA POWELL**

---

1. http://www.yourwebsite.com/

# Disclaimer

This is a work of fiction. Unless otherwise indicated, all the names, characters, businesses, places, events and incidents in this book are either the product of the author's imagination or used in a fictitious manner. Any resemblance to actual persons, living or dead, or actual events is purely coincidental.

# DEDICATION

This book is dedicated to my spouse.
LOVE YOU ALWAYS

# PROLOGUE

## July 26, 2016

Gail listened as the minister asked, "Is there anyone here that objects to this marriage?" There were no objections. She sat in the front row of the church with empty chairs all around her. She dabbed her eyes as she looked at the couple standing in front of the minster. The couple was her sister Tracie and her girlfriend Jody Jones. Jody's mom refused to acknowledge their relationship and refused to come. She said it was against her religious beliefs that two women should be together and marriage was definitely out of the question.

Tracie and Jody had already been living together for a year when gay marriage was legalized on June 26, 2015. One year later, they decided to take their relationship to the next level and marry.

The minister turned toward Tracie and said "Now we will hear the vows and have the exchange of rings

"I, Tracie, promise to love you more each day than the day before. I will rub your feet when they're cold and feed you chicken soup when you're sick. I will always take care of you and listen to your complaints. From this day forward I will try to be the best I can be. Always and Forever.." Tracie took Jody's hand and put a one carat diamond ring on her finger

The minister turned to Jody.

"I, Jody, promise to love you through the good and bad. I promise to give you the best of me now and always. Our love has been planted and like a tree I will water it with love and tenderness every day of my life." Jody took Tracie's hand and put a gold wedding band with diamonds circling it on her ring finger.

Gail reached in her purse and took out another tissue. Listening to the vows they said to each other kept her tears flowing. It was just the two of them; their parents had died a few years ago. They were not just sisters, but best friends too.

"You may kiss your spouse," The minister said.

Tracie and Jody came together and had a kiss so long that the minister had to clear his throat.

"Congratulations," Gail said walking toward them. She kissed each of them on the cheek.

When the minster came up to congratulate them Gail stood back and looked at the loving couple. When she first met Jody, it was evident why Tracie loved her. Jody was a lawyer, smart with a great sense of humor. When you saw them together you could see the love they had for each other shining in their eyes. She wished her marriage could have had a fraction of their love. Once the ceremony was over, Tracie and Jody headed to the airport for their two-week honeymoon in Cancun.

# AUGUST 2016

# Morning Love

Tracie awoke laying in bed, listening to the birds outside. She enjoyed the soft glow of the sunlight streaming through the window as she watched Jody sleeping.

Jody stirred, and turned toward her, whispering, "Take me."

Tracie knew that most mornings, her spouse's desire for her to bring her to an orgasm was powerful.

Jody's sex drive was off the chart and for the last six years, Tracie had been hypnotized by it.

Jody gazed at her with heavy lidded eyes and began to massage her own breast. "You want this?" she asked. "Then take it."

Unable to resist, Tracie kissed her long and hard then moved her mouth to her awaiting breast, kissing through her top. "I always want you, baby," she said, beginning to undress her, needing to feel her bare flesh

But a knock at the door halted her. "Mommies, I'm hungry." Sam, their six-year-old daughter said. The knob jiggled as she tried to enter. She was spunky and inquisitive no matter what time of day it was.

"Please give us a minute, Sunshine and I'll be right out to make you something." Tracie called out. She felt Jody shifting beside her and could tell by her body language she still was aching for her touch.

"I'm hungry," Sam said again in a whiney voice.

Tracie did what most parents of a kindergarten-aged child did. She tried reasoning. "Sam, count to twenty-five. When you say twenty-five call me, and I'll come out and make anything you want for breakfast."

"Okay," Sam said happily.

Tracie heard her run from the door.

When she was sure she was gone she slipped her hand inside Jody's panties and fingered her soaking wet vagina. She rubbed Jody's slippery clit between her fingers. She kissed her and whispered, "She'll be back soon."

Jody was breathless with need. "I know. But I want some mommy time."

Tracie pulled Jody's panties off and opened her legs wide so she could put her whole face in Jody's vagina. The smell of Jody was hypnotic. She flicked Jody's clit back and forth with her tongue while squeezing her nipples. Tracie could tell by the thrashing around she was doing that she was getting ready to climax. Then all of a sudden Jody arched her back and Tracie could taste the sweet juices of Jody's orgasm. They laid there for a while enjoying the after feeling of lovemaking; neither of them could say a word. Tracie came back to reality when she heard Sam calling her.

"Hey, whose turn to make breakfast?" Tracie said.

"You already told her you would," Jody said with a playful smile. "Besides, I need a little more time."

"Enjoy, but not too much without me." Tracie grinned. She knew Jody was going to touch herself, but there was nothing she could do. Sam had to eat. Tracie walked to the door opened it and looked back at her. She was lying there massaging her breast and grinding against her hand. Tracie could see how much she still needed her when she looked into her eyes. Tracie moved her eyes down her body all five foot six inches of her chocolate-colored skin. She was one hundred forty pounds of woman.

Regrettably, Tracie pulled the door closed, leaving Jody on her own. Walking to the kitchen she thought back to one of their conversations they had about adopting.

"Trace, please baby, you will be a great mother. It's not just you raising a child, it's us." Jody had said.

"I know, but suppose I'm not as great as you think I'll be?"

"I wouldn't bring a child into our family if I thought you couldn't handle it."

"Jody, you know I love you and I'll do anything for you, anything but..." Tracie said as her voice trailed off.

Jody looked her straight in her eyes. "You can, and we will be the greatest parents. You trust me?"

"Of course, with my life."

"Then give me this, not just for me, but for us."

"No" was a word Tracie found hard to say to Jody. "Okay, I guess we're adopting a baby." She said sheepishly.

Tracie had agreed to adoption, but she had made as many excuses as she could to prevent moving forward. There were many discussions of how and when it should take place; Jody wasn't backing down. She was confidant that it would happen. Tracie, on the other hand, kept saying she was ready, but inside motherhood scared her. She didn't feel she had any motherly instincts. When she saw babies, she didn't get that warm gooey feeling of wanting a child. Tracie figured something was wrong with her. She could only imagine how lonely Jody must have been, being an only child. She had Gail and couldn't imagine growing up without her. She could tell there was an emptiness in Jody that she couldn't fill, and for that reason Tracie filled out the paperwork with Jody to co- adopt just before their wedding.

The process had been long and trying, like buying a first house. When Jody saw Samantha's picture, she'shouted, "That's her, that's our daughter!" And when Tracie had looked at the picture of four-year-old Samantha, all smiles with chocolate Hershey-like skin, she too knew at that moment that their family was complete. She looked at Jody and grinned so hard it hurt. She finally felt the gooey feeling of motherhood that had always escaped her. Sam was the second best person to come into her life.

Tracie entered the kitchen and found Sam sitting at the table. "Okay, Sunshine, what's it going to be?"

After much thought Sam said, "Eggs, bacon and milk."

Tracie laughed a little at her certainty then prepared her meal. She laid out Sam's clothes for school while she ate, then sneaked off to check on Jody.

Opening the door softly, Tracie could see that Jody was fast asleep. She walked carefully to the bed and kissed her lips. Jody shifted under the covers. Tracie needed to feel her, if only for a minute. She took off her boxers and dove under the covers. She put her fingers between Jody's legs and felt the lingering wetness of her masturbation. Aroused, Tracie turned her over onto her back and mounted her. Then she writhed against Jody until she was fully awake and began to moan.

Jody held her tightly without opening her eyes. Tracie closed her eyes as well, to better enjoy the feel of their bodies together. It only took seconds before she felt herself shudder in climax. There was a dizziness that came over her from the intensity of the orgasm.

With her head spinning and her heart pounding, she could only lean over and kiss Jody long and hard. "I love you more than life itself," she whispered.

"I love you, too," Jody said softly.

They heard Sam trying to open the locked door.

"Go get dressed, Sweetie and don't forget to put lotion on those elbows and knees," Tracie yelled through the closed door.

Jody piped in as well. "Don't forget to put your pencils in your book bag."

"Okay," Sam said through the door.

Tracie gave Jody one last kiss and got up to shower and dress. She thought of how happy they were as she showered. She never knew love could feel so good. They were a family.

# Tha Accident

Jody was driving to work, beaming from the great sex she'd had an hour ago with the person she couldn't imagine her life without. She had a great job at a law firm downtown in New York City as an advocator for children. Her love for children came from her being an only child and not really having time to have many friends growing up. Their family moved often with her father being in the military, friendships were very few. She didn't show it, but the loneliness she felt left a hole inside her. Jody did well in school; from elementary through law school, she was a star. She made her parents proud. When she thought of marriage, children were always part of the picture. She didn't want just one because she didn't want her child to go through the loneliness that she had felt. She was overjoyed when Tracie finally said yes.She now had the best family anyone could ask for. Jody knew she wasn't perfect; when she got mad, she would shut down. She couldn't deal with not being in control of situations and when she felt she wasn't in control, she fought back with a vengeance.. She couldn't believe that someone would love her so unconditionally asTracie did.

"Now, if I could only get out this damn traffic," she said to herself.

The next thing she felt was her car being pushed to the side. She held onto the wheel. She could hear voices all around her, but she couldn't open her eyes or speak. She could hear the faint sound of an ambulance siren before completely blacking out.

***

Tracie managed to get Sam to the school bus and see Jody off to work with a long, lingering kiss. She was sitting in Starbucks with her favorite mocha coffee and newspaper, waiting to start her school day. She taught gym at the local junior high school. Her work hours varied, which allowed time to see both Sam and Jody off before she had to leave for work. She was about to take her second sip of coffee when her iPhone rang. *Who the hell is calling me this early?* she thought, scowling at the unknown number.

"Hello?"

"May I speak with Tracie Davis?" The voice was unfamiliar and professional.

"Yes. Who's calling?" She replied with curiosity.

"My name is Janet Murphy. I'm calling from Mount Sinai Hospital."

Tracie stood, nearly knocking over her coffee. What was wrong? Something was wrong. Her heart nearly came out of her chest. *What is a hospital calling me for?* Her thoughts were jumbled up inside of her. Then she heard the voice on the other end say.

"Do you know a Jody Jones?"

"I know Jody Jones. I'm on my way." She said running to her car not waiting to hear all the facts.

Tracie knew where the hospital was, so she didn't bother to ask. Her mind was racing, wondering what Jody was doing at the hospital. Why couldn't she call herself? Did she want to know? Probably not. Oh God, please don't let it be bad. She drove erratically through New York City morning traffic. She thought back to that morning, of making love to Jody and cooking Sam's breakfast. Life was good. And now, a little over an hour later...her thought trailed off, not daring to continue.

Tracie parked in front of the emergency room entrance. She ran in through the automatic doors. She stopped at the first desk she saw.

Her words came tumbling out. "I'm here about Jody Jones I got a phone call to come here. My name is Tracie Davis. She's my spouse."

"Have a seat. Someone will be with you in a minute." The receptionist seemed disinterested and mechanical-like.

Tracie refused to listen to that bullshit with Jody lying somewhere needing her. She couldn't believe this woman was sitting there looking at her like she was being disturbed. "Excuse me, but I want to see someone now. Not in a minute, but now." Tracie looked at her with her eyes blazing. She started to adjust her body to get in a more aggressive stance.

The woman behind the desk sucked her teeth as she picked up the telephone to page the doctor. "Have a seat," she said with the same disinterested manner.

Tracie was too nervous to sit so she paced the length of the waiting area for what seemed like hours.

Then a voice on the loudspeaker called her name.

Tracie ran to the desk as fast as she could without knocking over anyone in her way. "I'm here about Jody Jones," she said nervously.

A man in scrubs addressed her. "I'm Doctor Bernard." He didn't offer a hand in greeting.

"I have to ask what relationship are you to Jody Jones?"

"I'm her spouse, Tracie Davis. What's going on? Is she hurt?" This was one of the reasons she and Jody had decided to get married: so they could be there for each other no matter the situation. They both carried their marriage certificate with them always. Her stomach flip-flopped seeing the look on his face; it wasn't good.

"Do you have some proof of your relationship?

"Yeah, here." Tracie pulled the marriage certificate from her pocket and shoved it in his face. "Now, can you please tell me what's going on?"

The doctor looked at the certificate and handed it back. "She has been in a car accident. We are examining her now to get the full extent of her injuries. I'll be able to tell you more when we've finished. Have a seat and I'll come to talk to you as soon as we're done."

Tracie touched the doctor's arm as he was turning "Doctor that woman in there means everything to me."

"I understand, Ms. Davis." Then he turned on his heels and pushed through the swinging doors.

Tracie moved to a quiet corner to call Jody's mother. Her hand shook as she pressed the phone to her ear. The answering machine came on.

"Ms. Jones, this is Tracie. There has been some kind of accident involving Jody. Please come to Mount Sinai Hospital in Manhattan."

She ended the call and hoped she'd sounded calm enough. Jody's mother had heart problems and she worried how she would handle all this.

Tracie went back outside and paced in front of the hospital. She realized that with the air conditioner noise she might not hear her name being called. She went back inside and sat toward the back, away from other people. She couldn't believe she was sitting in a hospital. She couldn't bear the thought that she could lose Jody. She clenched and unclenched her hands, a sign of nervousness. As she sat there, she started to think about all the things they still had to do, like seeing Sam go to college, vacationing in Paris and buying the house they've been saving for. Tracie's eyes began to tear. She spotted Ms. Jones maneuvering her way through people standing in the waiting room.

"Where's the doctor?" Ms. Jones barked as she neared Tracie. "Have you heard anything new? Have you talked to the doctor?" Her face was ashen with sweat beading down her forehead. She looked as terrified as Tracie felt.

She was a retired schoolteacher who still spoke with conviction and expected others to hop to her every word. Tracie was suddenly thankful for it all.

Ms. Jones kept smoothing down her purple Hanes sweat suit as she looked hurriedly around the waiting room.

She was a bundle of nerves.

Tracie spoke, trying to sound calm. "The doctor's name is Dr Bernard. He'll speak with us as soon as he finishes examining her. He said she was in some kind of car accident."

"How long has it been?" She hurried to the counter, not giving Tracie time to respond.

The doctor appeared at the receptionist desk just as Ms. Jones was starting to lay into the receptionist. He looked grim.

Tracie hurried to the receptionist desk.

"Dr. Bernard this is Jody's mother, Ms. Jones."

He nodded his head to acknowledge her. "Why don't we go over here so we can speak privately." He took Ms. Jones's arm and guided her toward the back of the emergency room waiting area.

Tracie followed, the three of them moving as one. Tracie sat next to Ms. Jones and theld her hand for support.

"Please tell me what's going on with my baby," Ms. Jones said, her voice cracking a little.

Tracie squeezed her hand.

The doctor looked at them sympathetically. "Your daughter was brought here after a car accident on the West Side Highway. After examination we found she has a broken left arm, bruised ribs, and a very big gash on her head. I had the neurologist examine her and, there seems to be no brain damage that he can see at this time. That's all I can tell you right now. We're giving her the best care possible."

"When will you know more?" Ms. Jones asked.

"The next forty-eight hours are crucial. We will continue to monitor her brain activity, but we won't know anything for certain until she wakes up."

"She's not awake?" Tracie asked, her heart sinking.

"No, she's still unconscious."

"Oh my God." Ms. Jones said.

"Can we see her now?" Tracie asked weakly.

"Yes, just for a few minutes. She needs her rest." The doctor rose to take them down the hall to Jody's room.

Tracie had a thousand questions in her mind. but no words came out. She clenched and unclenched her hand. *Is this nightmare ever going to end?* she wondered as she walked to Jody's room.

"Please only stay a minute," Dr. Bernard said as he showed them into Jody's room.

The lights were dim. They could see the faint outline of Jody's body lying in bed. Tracie and Ms. Jones walked over to her, and each took a hand.

Tracie, spoke, but it wasn't easy. "Baby, it's me and your mother. We're here everything is going to be alright."

There was no movement from Jody. Seeing her nearly lifeless body tore Ms. Jones's heart out. It had been just the two of them since Jody was 16 years old. She loved Jody very much though they had their differences especially about her being gay. Their relationship became strained when Jody told her about her relationship with Tracie. Ms. Jones wished she'd kept her mouth shut and her opinions to herself. She didn't understand what one woman could see romantically in another woman, and she'd expressed this often to Jody. Now, seeing her laying there, none of that mattered. If only she would open her eyes, she would tell that her happiness was all that mattered.

The nurse came in just as they turned to leave. She put her hand on Ms. Jones shoulder as if to say everything is going to be alright.

They walked through the swinging doors, a waterfall of tears falling from their eyes. They sat for a minute on a waiting room bench, then gathered themselves to leave

Ms. Jones dabbed her eyes and managed to whisper. "She didn't move."

Tracie noticed her tremble and steadied her. Tracie was afraid this might be too much for Ms. Jones's heart condition. "Let me take you home so you can rest."

"Rest? REST! My daughter is lying in that room unconscious, and you want me to rest."

Tracie knew this was hard on Jody's mother because it was damn near killing her. She squeezed her arm gently and reasoned with her to go home and lay down.

"Ms. Jones, what good are you going to be to Jody when she wakes up if you are sick? You have to remember your heart condition. I promise I will let you know the second she wakes up."

Tracie knew she wasn't going to go home and rest. She was going to come back and stay right there after taking Ms. Jones home. Sleep and peace of mind would both be far in coming. Sam came to mind, and she hurriedly wiped a warm tear away. She'd ask her sister to pick her up after school.

Ms. Jones saw her wiping her cheeks and meekly agreed to go home. The ride was very quiet, each with their thoughts. Tracie thought about the first time Jody took her to meet her mother.

"She'll like you," Jody said to ease her nervousness.

Tracie was still scared to death... They'd been dating about six months, and it was getting serious. They had started talking about living together and the responsibilities that came with it. Jody told her that she came out to her mother a few months before this, and it didn't go well. Her mother refused to believe she could love a woman. She started reciting passages from

**Romans 1:26-27 NIV**

**"Because of this, God gave them over to shameful lusts. Even their women exchanged natural sexual relations for unnatural ones. In the same way the men also abandoned natural relations with women and were inflamed with lust for one another. Men committed shameful acts with other men and received in themselves the due penalty for their error."**

Jody said she just got up and left. They didn't speak for almost a whole month after that conversation. Jody had begged and pleaded with her mother to just meet Tracie and she'd see why she was in love with her. Jody's mother finally said yes to a dinner but only if Jody gave this lesbian thing some more thought and not make up her mind so quickly. Jody hadn't told her mother that she was dating women before Tracie. The men she saw Jody with were staged dates.

What do you have on your feet?" Jody asked, laughing as she looked down at Tracie's feet.

"Socks and shoes."

Jody was growing more hysterical. "What color are your socks?"

"Bluuueee," Tracie said before looking down. "Oh shit!" When Tracie looked down, she saw one navy and one black sock. What the fuck? Jody, pull over at any store you pass. Hell, look what time it is. We're already late, forget it. I just won't wear any socks." But she couldn't do that. Frustrated, she walked in wearing a light blue suit with dark mis- matching socks and black suede shoes.

To her horror, Ms. Jones noticed when she sat. "A new look?"

Tracie looked down pretending that she didn't know about her socks. She tried to play it off with some lame joke, but it was lost on Ms. Jones. So, Tracie sat in silence the rest of the meal and only spoke when spoken to.

That dinner set the tone for all their meetings. She was invisible. Tracie realized she would never be anything but a gym teacher to Ms. Jones, someone below Jody's standards. That thought always brought about a cold anger, but she was so in love with Jody that she refused to let a judgmental woman like Ms. Jones interfere in their relationship. Ms. Jones never would think anyone was good enough for Jody, especially a woman.

Tracie dropped off Ms. Jones, promising to call with any change, then called her sister.

When her sister answered on the third ring, she almost lost it. The words burst out of her mouth. "Gail, Jody is in the hospital, and I need you to pick up Sam."

"Sure, what's going on?" Gail asked starting to get nervous.

"It's, it's Jody!" Tracie stammered trying to get the words out more clearly.

"What happened?"

"There was some kind of car accident. Jody is unconscious and that's all we know," she said almost in tears. The emotions that Tracie felt could finally come out.

"Hey, don't cry. Do you need me to come down? I'm not doing anything."

"No, please just pickup Sam and let her stay with you tonight. I want to be here in case Jody wakes up." She didn't want to impose any more than she had to; Gail was going through her own mess. A messy divorce.

***

Gail's husband, Richard, was a CEO of a corporation on Wall Street. Gail was a housewife, tending to his every demand. They had no children, but Gail had hoped to have some in the future. Gail's life changed one day when a young woman turned up at her door. She informed Gail that she was from Virginia and had been sleeping with Richard for over a year. The worst part was when she told Gail she was pregnant.

When Gail confronted her husband about it, he at first started to lie, but then the truth came out. He told her he was moving to Virginia and wanted a divorce. That was the last time she had seen or spoken directly to him. They only communicated through lawyers. She had signed a pre-nup that she was contesting on the grounds that he coerced her.

The bastard was sneaky in getting her to sign the pre-nup. He made it seem like a pre-nup was a standard formality, like a bank account. He said it was more for her benefit so she wouldn't lose anything in case of divorce. The way he put it even though she didn't have much a court would give him half because they lived in a community property state. If a judge was going to give her half of his and he was going to get half of hers they might as well keep what they had. Gail was naïve.

She was in love, and she trusted him. He had taken her on a romantic weekend in the country. She had been in awe of the surroundings and had relaxed, maybe a little too much. One evening, after she had drunk a little too much champagne, he said they could really enjoy themselves if they didn't have to worry about the pre-nup hanging over their heads. He then put the papers in front of her and she signed while he nibbled her neck. After all their years of marriage she never really knew what the papers said—until this started, and she had her lawyer get a copy from his lawyer.

She never mentioned to Tracie what happened because she felt stupid and ashamed.

Gail put her anger aside. "Okay, if you need anything else, let me know. I'll pick up a few things of Sam's from the apartment in case she needs to stay awhile." She paused. "I know this is hard. Jody's gonna be fine."

Tracie swallowed her pain. "Thanks, sis. I'll call you to check on Sam later."

She went back to the waiting area. The clock on the wall seemed to stand still. The only time she could remember waiting for something this important was when she and Jody waited to hear about their adoption of Sam. Tracie, like Jody, hated not being in control. It made her feel so helpless. She moved from chair to chair. She tried reading but couldn't focus. Nothing seemed to move the clock. She kept asking the receptionist with the bad attitude if there was any change in Jody's condition. The answer was always NO! Tracie wanted to wring her neck.

When night came, Tracie covered herself with a blanket from the trunk of her car and laid uncomfortably on the waiting room couch. She fell asleep, lost in the warm thoughts of their love making that very morning. It seemed like a century ago.

# The Hospital

Dr. Bernard went to Jody's room as soon as he started his shift. He was surprised when he walked in and saw her eyes open looking up at the ceiling.

"Where am I?" she asked slowly and softly upon seeing him.

"Good morning, Jody. My name is Dr. Bernard and you're in Mount Sinai hospital. You were in a car accident yesterday. How do you feel?"

Jody moved her head to look around. She timidly said, "I'm okay, I guess. I'm sore and my head hurts some."

"That's to be understood. I have some tests scheduled for you, so just rest. By the way, your mother and spouse are anxious to see you."

"Who?"

"Your mother, Ms. Jones, and your spouse, Tracie Davis. Do you know who they are?" He asked quizzically trying to understand her response.

"I don't remember anyone with those names?"

"Do you know your name is Jody?"

"Yes, of course I do."

Do you remember being in a car accident?

"No."

He asked a few more questions before going back to ask her about her mother and Tracie.

"But you don't remember anyone named Tracie or anything about your mother?"

"No, doctor I don't." She said getting upset. "When can I go home?"

"You'll go home soon, but for now I want you to rest. Someone should be by after breakfast for your test. Our psychologist Dr. Stable will also be by to see you later this afternoon. I'll check on you later."

Dr. Bernard, walking past the waiting room, saw Tracie sleeping. He woke her. "Have you been here all night?" He appeared to be freshly showered and Tracie could smell his soap mixing with the coffee brewing nearby.

She sat up, suddenly very awake. "I'm not leaving until I know she's okay," she said defiantly.

"Well, I've just seen her and she's awake."

Tracie broke out in a big smile. "Thank you."

He went on speaking. "The bruises should heal nicely along with the broken bones. But I'm afraid that's the only good news I have."

"What do you mean?"

"Jody may have amnesia caused by a concussion. Concussions from car accidents are fairly common when there's been trauma to the head. She doesn't seem to remember anything of the accident. She knows who she is, but she doesn't respond correctly to some questions I asked. I have scheduled her for a CT scan so we can have another look at her brain. I don't want you to panic because these types of injuries can reverse on their own with time."

"Her memory?" Tracie asked not believing what she was hearing.

"Yes."

"You said she knows who she is?"

"Yes, but not some other things."

Tracie interrupted. "Like what?"

"Maybe you should see for yourself. Let me warn you, though, she might not know you.

"I can see her?" Tracie asked anxiously.

"Yes, but only for a few minutes," he said.

Tracie slowly started her walk to the other end of the long hall beyond the swinging doors. She was nervous and scared, not knowing what to expect from Jody. She was startled by the sounds of a woman yelling from a room just ahead of her. She couldn't help but look in. There was a crowd of doctors surrounding her bed, and the woman looked as if she was sitting up. Her yelling persisted. Tracie briefly wondered what that was all about, but she had her own problem to deal with a couple of doors down. She continued her slow pace to the room.

"Hey," she said softly after she knocked and entered Jody's room.

Jody looked at her blankly. Tracie thought it might be the pain killers they had probably given her. Jody tugged up the covers as if for protection and reached for the nurse's button. Tracie knew something was definitely wrong. Jody had a blank expression on her face.

Jody asked, "Who are you?"

"I'm Tracie, your spouse. Don't you know me, Jody?"

Dr. Bernard and one of the floor nurses had followed her down the hallway. They stood in the doorway watching the exchange between Jody and Tracie.

"Take it slow," Dr. Bernard said.

Tracie looked across the room to see the other bed was empty and there was only a telephone on the table. She felt a little better knowing that she could speak freely without any funny glances from a roommate.

Jody looked to the doctor as if for clues. Then she answered. "No."

Tracie was shocked. She didn't know what to say; her legs nearly buckled.

"I-I wanted to see how you are." Tracie jumbled words came out.

"I'm okay." Jody answered not sure of what to say.

Tracie fumbled for her wallet. "I have some pictures that might help you remember me."

Jody looked at her with tears falling. "I'm sorry but I don't remember you. Please I'm tired. Can you come back another time."

"Please Jody, look at the pictures and here's our marriage license. You have a whole life before the accident. We have an adopted daughter named Sam. I know this might be hard for you to understand, but you were in an accident and," Tracie words trailed off; she felt helpless.

Jody laid down and closed her eyes. She felt overwhelmed with everything that was going on.

The nurse, seeing Jody agitated, stepped into the room. She spoke to Tracie. "Ms. you are going to have to leave now. She needs her rest."

Tears formed in Tracie's eyes. She felt like her best friend had died. She was too hurt and shocked to say anything. She placed the photos and marriage license on Jody's bed table.

"When you get a chance, look at the pictures and license." Tracie said in a whisper.

She was afraid her emotions would get the best of her if she spoke any louder. She felt hurt and confused by their interaction. She left the room and closed the door softly behind her.

Tracie saw Ms. Jones sitting on a bench in the ER and wondered how long she'd been there. She sat down beside her and said softly, "She didn't know me."

Ms. Jones sighed. "I need to go in and see her." She hesitated, and Tracie could tell she was fearful.

They sat there for a few minutes trying to console each other. Tracie didn't know what they were going to do. She had no idea what was going to happen next. Eventually, Ms. Jones rose and headed down the hallway toward Jody's room. Tracie watched her go. She felt so helpless. She needed to get out of there as quickly as she could. She couldn't think straight. She figured Ms. Jones would take a car service when she didn't see her.

***

Gail could tell by Tracie's voice on the phone that the day had been hard. "How's Jody? Where are you?"

"I'm on my way to your house. I just wanted to make sure you were home. It's been rough, Gail really rough." Tears immediately started pouring down Tracie's face. She needed to pull over before she had an accident. She jerked the wheel to the right into the first spot she saw.

"Gail, she didn't know me. I was a complete stranger. You should have seen how she looked at me," Tracie said wiping away the tears.

"Whaat?" Gail said with disbelief.

"It was awful, Gail. I can't believe this is happening. I just don't know what to do." There was a long pause while Gail chose her words. "Trace, you have to be strong. Remember, there's a little girl that needs you no matter what you're going through. Is there anything I can do?"

"Yeah, it might be better if we stayed at your house until this is over. At least we can all be there for each other. Why don't you pick up Sam and I'll go pick up things that we might need from the apartment."

"Sounds good," Gail said.

Tracie could hear weariness in Gail's voice. "Did you see your lawyer today? I'm so sorry, Gail, to be dumping all this on you. I know you have your own problems."

"Yeah, I saw him. He said that bastard wants me to sell the house."

"Are you kidding me? You sure you're okay with us being there?"

Tracie knew that Gail was mad as hell that her soon-to-be-ex-husband would want her to sell their house. It wasn't like he needed the money or anything.

Gail had spent so many years catering to his needs that she had no life of her own; she lived on an allowance that he gave her weekly. According to him, "my money is mine and this is what you get." Tracie felt bad for her, knowing the only friends Gail had were his friends. Tracie was pretty much her best friend as well as her sister. They needed each other now more than any time since their parents died.

"I'm good with this, plus I get to spend some quality time with my niece. I'll pick up Sam and some takeout and we'll meet you at the house."

Tracie drove to her apartment slowly to get her thoughts together. She had to tell Sam about Jody, and that was going to be hard. She entered the dark apartment with that on her mind and turned on only the hallway light. She sat down at the table and cried. The cry came from down deep in her soul and it lasted for what seemed like hours.

Afterward, feeling mentally and physically drained, she poured herself a shot of tequila and downed it quickly. The burn was welcoming; it enabled her to start packing their clothes.

She took enough for a few days, unsure how long they'd need to stay with Gail.

She went to Sam's room, packed a few more items to make sure Sam would be comfortable.

***

Tracie knew Gail would take good care of Sam. She'd make sure her homework was done and do silly things that an aunt does to please her niece. This way, Tracie would be free to run back and forth to the hospital. She'd be able to stay as long as she wanted. She went into her and Jody's bedroom, and her eyes swelled with tears. She didn't know when they would enjoy snuggling under the covers again. She felt an emptiness inside herself. She hurriedly packed the rest of her clothes and rushed out before the feeling overtook her again.

"Mommy, Mommy," Sam said when she saw her in the open door.

"How's my favorite girl?" Tracie said putting a smile on her face.

"Fine! Auntie Gail said I'm gonna be staying with her for a little while." Sam's face took on a bewildered look. "Why?"

Tracie thought for a moment trying to find the best way to explain what had happened. She didn't want to make her scared. She was just 6 years old, and Tracie thought the truth was too much for her to understand. She was having a hard time herself.

"Well, there was an accident and Mommy Jody got hurt but she is going to be okay. I saw the doctor and he felt it was best for her to stay in the hospital for a little while."

"Why?" Sam asked confused.

"Well, he feels that way he can make doubly sure that she's okay before she comes home." She let that settle in then hugged her.

"Can I go to the hospital?" Sam asked hugging Tracie back.

"Sam, I'm sorry, they don't allow children in the hospital. When grownups are sick in the hospital, they need rest. It can be upsetting to children to see their mommies and daddies in there."

Sam seemed to consider this. "Okay, tell mommy I love her when you go back to the hospital."

"I will," Tracie said in a comforting tone while squeezing her tightly.

Sam loved Jody a lot. Tracie knew she was missing her already. She only hoped she had handled it well.

Dinner was pretty quiet except for their forks hitting their plates, which wasn't too often. After dinner they played a game of dress up with Sam until bedtime. Tracie could tell Sam was sad because she wasn't her usually bubbly self.

Tracie wanted Sam to understand that Jody would be home soon, and they needed to be strong. But maybe she was just trying to convince herself as much as Sam. Truthfully, she had no idea if Jody was going to be fine. If anything was going to be fine at all anymore.

Tracie tucked Sam into bed and laid down next to her. The sound of her sleeping was soothing.

Tracie closed her eyes and her mind drifted to that Thanksgiving night when she met Jody.

It was a cold night at a club called Slow Dance. Jody walked in wearing jeans, a silk blouse and fur coat. She was with two females. Tracie watched the way she moved through the crowd of pulsating bodies. Tracie felt like she was moving for her eyes only. She had refused everyone's offer of a dance and so did her friends. But the way she looked at Tracie drew her closer to her.

Tracie eased her five-foot–eight caramel frame over to where Jody was standing.

"Can I have this dance?" Tracie asked, a bit timid.

Jody looked Tracie up and down. She thought "not bad... dreads, caramel colored skin, rugged build and a nice dresser."

"Sure."

The song that happened to come on was a slow one. They held each other tightly. They looked into each other's eyes as if they could see deep into the other's soul. The music stopped but they didn't until they were in Tracie's apartment tearing each other's clothes off.

Tracie held her and looked into her eyes. Jody took her hand and let Tracie lead without words being spoken. They just went with the cravings of their bodies. Jody's was soaked with the anticipation of Tracie's touch. Tracie laid Jody on her bed and opened her legs. Jody was eager for her to enter her with her tongue. Tracie slowly worked her way up her thighs to her center kissing every inch. She kissed and licked the walls of Jody's vagina causing her to move her hips. Tracie moved her hands up her stomach to her breast and squeezed her nipples, causing her to exhale and groan.

Then Tracie flicked Jody's clit back and forth with her tongue. She was so wet Tracie had to lick some of the juices from her first in order to feel the softness of her clit. Then she put her clit between the gap in her teeth to hold it while she licked harder. She put two fingers inside her and pumped

"Hmmm, that is good," Jody whispered as Tracie pumped faster. She couldn't stop the sounds that escaped her mouth.

Tracie was so intoxicated with pleasing her she almost gave in and sent her into a climax.

Wanting the night to last forever, she slowed the pace down.

Gently, she slowed her fingers inside her and gently sucked her clit. The feeling was too much for Jody's body to withstand without reacting. She held onto Tracie's shoulders and moved her hips faster.

Tracie moved her fingers faster to meet the movement of Jody's hips, cringing in sweet pain as Jody's nails dug down into her shoulders.

"That's so good. Give it to me baby," Jody whispered between breaths.

She knew Jody was getting ready to come so she applied more pressure, and felt her juices run down her fingers. Tracie looked up at her face and there a was peacefulness to her. She moved up and held her in her arms. Tracie drifted off to sleep with those memories to comfort her.

# Tracie and Ms Jones At The Hospital

Early the next morning, Tracie was headed to the hospital after an early call from Ms. Jones. The doctor was anxious to see them, and Tracie was anxious as hell to hear what he had to say. She picked up Ms. Jones.

"She didn't remember me, either," Ms. Jones said softly shortly after she eased into Tracie's car.

"I'm sorry."

"Lord so am I."

Tracie watched her retrieve a tissue and dab at her eyes. Her chest shook as sobs overtook her. Tracie's eyes began to fill with tears. She reached over and touched Ms. Jones's hand. Ms. Jones took Tracie's hand in hers and squeezed it. They were bonded in their grief.

They had the doctor paged as soon as they arrived. When he came through the swinging doors, he took Ms. Jones by the arm and led them to a corner. They sat on the hard waiting room chairs.

He took off his glasses and put them in his white doctor's coat pocket. He leaned in close and spoke in a low but reassuring tone. "The CT scan came back without showing any brain damage."

Tracie sighed loudly with relief. Ms. Jones stifled back more sobs as the doctor continued.

"However, concussion victims don't usually have amnesia to the extent Jody does. The fact she isn't remembering the accident is quite normal along with some short-term loss of what happened shortly before the accident is called retrograde amnesia. But Jody's memory loss extends beyond that. She has a very unusual case in that her memory is selective. Right now, there aren't any concrete answers I can give you as to when she'll remember each of you. The only thing I can suggest at this point is to talk to her about her favorite things and bring pictures for her to look at. Hopefully, she will remember something. Other than that, we just have to wait."

"Is that all we can do, just sit and wait?" Tracie looked at the doctor with tears in her eyes as she tried to process all he had said. She realized that her life might not be the same for a very long time.

The doctor gently touched her shoulder. "I have asked Dr. Stable, a psychologist on staff here, to spend some time with Jody. I am hoping that by her talking about the things she does remember that other memories will surface. Let me reiterate: selective amnesia is unusual, and Jody does have some recognition and memories. Dr Stable has met Jody a few times."

"Can we see her?" Ms. Jones weakly asked.

"Sure. But make it brief."

They rose and walked slowly through the swinging door, maneuvering around carts and nurses doing their morning rounds. No one spoke, they just watched as nurses stopped to speak to Dr. Bernard. When they reached Jody's door, the doctor entered first. Tracie and Ms. Jones followed him in but stood near the door, unsure whether to come in. Tracie's heart was beating so fast she thought it might explode. She was scared that she would be rejected again. Ms. Jones was equally afraid of how Jody would respond to her. She started sweating profusely from the anticipation.

"Hello, Dr. Stable. Hello, Jody. How are you today?" Dr. Bernard asked.

Jody said okay but nothing more. She was sitting up in her bed with the covers pulled to her breast. The blank look on her face showed nothing. The tray with her breakfast was pushed to the side uneaten. Tracie and Ms. Jones came to where the two doctors were standing.

"Ms. Jones, this is Dr. Stable the psychologist I spoke about in the hallway."

Dr. Stable extended her hand to Ms. Jones. "Nice to meet you."

"Dr. Stable, this is Jody's spouse Tracie."

Dr. Bernard went on to say, "Dr. Stable will be trying to help Jody regain her memory."

***

Dr. Stable turned toward Tracie. "Hello, nice to meet you. May I speak to you in the hall for a minute?"

Tracie followed Dr. Stable out of the room.

"I understand from Dr. Bernard that Jody is your spouse?"

"Yes, that right."

"I've spoken to Jody briefly about your relationship. She has no memory of being married to a woman. That part of her memory has been wiped clean from the accident. She honestly believes she's a heterosexual person. Jody has told me about her growing up and that her mother was very religious. I surmised that her strong feeling against being gay has come from her childhood because she grew up in a very religious family. You might not like what I'm going to suggest, but I think for right now that we don't push the fact of you being her spouse It might be easier for her to remember your relationship if she gets to know you as a friend.

"I know this is hard for you but if we go slow with Jody, I feel she could get her memory back.

It is up to you whether you'll go along with this, of course. If you don't want to, I'll find another way.

I do feel this will be the quickest way to get her back to the Jody you used to know before the accident.

Tracie took a minute to digest what the doctor was asking her to do. "I'll do anything to get her back to the way she was. I'll play the friend. I do have one question—what about our marriage license? Does she think its fake or something?

"I did ask her about it when I saw it with pictures on her table. She didn't have a definitive answer about it. Jody implied, as you said, a fake. I asked why would you give her a fake marriage license and her response was she didn't know. I didn't push any further because she was getting agitated."

"Okay, Thank you."

"Thank you." Dr. Stable said as they walked back into the room,

Dr. Stable turned to Ms. Jones. "I'm glad that you came when you did. I was just about to tell Jody what to expect going forward." She turned from person to person as she spoke. "I will have two sessions a week with her. It will be in my office downstairs on the sixth floor. We will talk about anything that she wants. I'm hoping that a certain event in her thoughts will trigger another realization for her."

Tracie spoke before Ms. Jones had a chance. "So that's it! That's your plan?"

Dr. Bernard faced Tracie. "I know you want miracles, but there are none. We have no control over how long it will take her brain to put things in order. We only can do our best to help it along. You have to prepare yourselves for what may be a long process.

"That's fine, but I was hoping for more," said Tracie slowly.

"Try to be patient," Dr. Stable said. "I know it's difficult."

There was a brief silence before both doctors excused themselves with polite smiles and whispered goodbyes.

Tracie moved closer to Jody's bed along with Ms. Jones. Neither seemed to know what to say.

"How are you today?" Ms. Jones finally asked.

"I'm fine."

"Do you know who Sam is?" Tracie asked though she knew what she'd just agreed to.

Jody's look let Tracie know that she didn't have a clue of what she was talking about.

"She's your daughter and she loves and misses you. I was thinking that we'd take that trip to Paris as soon as you're up to it."

"She's my daughter?" Jody whispered

"Yes, she is." Tracie said hoping this would trigger something.

Ms. Jones chimed enthusiastically. "Isn't that nice, baby, Paris?"

Jody didn't respond; she just stared straight ahead. Ms. Jones reached out her hand to touch her, but Jody only jerked away.

Ms. Jones tried talking to her again. "When you get out of here, I'm going to make some of my famous fried chicken that you love so much."

"Please leave. I've had enough for one day."

"Well, I guess we should let you rest," Ms. Jones said, feeling defeated.

Tracie turned to leave with Ms. Jones but turned back to look at Jody. "See you tomorrow."

Jody didn't know these people and she felt overwhelmed by them. It was bad enough she had no memory of some of the things asked by doctors, but a child and married to a woman was too much. Jody felt frustrated and scared. Frustrated that she couldn't remember and scared about a life they kept saying she had. She laid down and turned over.

***

They walked slowly down the hall toward the swinging door leading into the waiting room, oblivious to the rustle of nurses pushing IV poles and patients in wheelchairs trying to maneuver in the hall. They sat in the first two seats they could find.

"Lord, what do we do now?" Ms. Jones said.

Tracie looked at Ms. Jones. She looked like she had aged ten years. "I don't know. We just have to hope they know what they're doing."

There was more bustling around them as they sat in silence. Tracie felt a helplessness she hadn't felt since her parents died.

"Let me take you home," she said forcing herself into action.

They settled in the car Tracie started to turn on the radio but instead turned to Ms. Jones'

"Have you been eating?"

"I've been eating. I have medicine to take so I eat. Who's taking care of Sam while you're at the hospital so often?"

"We're staying with my sister Gail so I can be at the hospital as much as I want. Gail's good with Sam."

"Does Sam know what happened to Jody?"

The stopped at a light and Tracie turned toward Ms. Jones. "I told Sam as much as I thought she could handle. Ms. Jones, I know how you feel about me and Jody, but I want you to know I love your daughter more than life itself. I'll be at the hospital everyday all day."

Tracie started driving and pulled up to Ms. Jones house. Ms. Jones didn't get out

"Tracie, I have nothing against you personally. I want you to know that. I love my grandbaby. I want you to know that it's just the way you and Jody are living is something against what I believe. If something happens to Jody, I don't know what I'll do. All this lesbian stuff right now is not important to me. I just want Jody to get better.

Tracie got out walked to Ms. Jones side of the car and opened the door. She helped Ms. Jones out and walked her to the front door of the house. Once Ms. Jones had opened the door Tracie reached up and kissed her cheek.

"Goodnight, Ms. Jones."

Ms. Jones was startled by the peck on the cheek "Goodnight Tracie."

Tracie got back in her car and stared at the small ranch style house. She knew Ms. Jones loved Jody, and this was a difficult situation for any mother. Tracie didn't doubt that Ms. Jones loved Sam because she never missed the chance to send a toy store of presents to her. The distance she kept from them was something a lot of older people did when having a gay family member; their religious beliefs didn't allow them to understand anyone being gay.

The houses in the neighborhood were all of the same type except in color. Ms. Jones's house was blue with white trim. There was a little yard in the front and back big enough to mow, but not enough for the sit-down kind of mower. `It was quiet with mostly elderly people who probably brought their houses when they were starting out.

Tracie decided to drive around Central Park to clear her head. There were always people in Central Park no matter the weather. The trees were plentiful, and the park stretched for miles in all directions. You could jog, lay on the grass eat your lunch in the summer, and in winter kids liked to go sliding down the many hills. It was a place that Tracie could be alone, but not really alone, when needed. She drove for nearly thirty minutes trying to clear her head. Then it was time to go. She had told Gail she'd pick Sam up from the bus.

***

"Mommy, Mommy!" Sam yelled when she saw Tracie walking toward the bus. She ran toward Tracie at full speed. Tracie swooped her up while planting kisses on her chubby cheeks.

"I thought Auntie Gail was picking me up," she said excited.

"Well, I told Auntie Gail that we'd see her at home for dinner. How was school?"

"OooKay." Sam grinned showing her two missing front teeth. "Did you see mommy today?" she asked.

"Yes, I did."

"Did you tell her that I love her?" Sam asked, fidgeting.

She put Sam down and they started walking to the car parked down the street.

"Yes, I did."

Tracie hated lying but she feared a little girl Sam's age wouldn't understand all that was happening. She thought it would only scare her.

"She told me to tell you she loves you too and that she hopes she will be home soon."

When they reached the car, she made sure Sam was secure in her seatbelt before going around to the driver's side and securing herself. Sam talked non-stop on the ride to Gail's.

Tracie welcomed the distraction so she wouldn't think of Jody.

When they arrived at the house, Gail was in the kitchen finishing up a much-needed home cooked meal. The aroma of seafood made Tracie's mouth water. She could tell by the smell it was paella with rice, a favorite of hers. Jody would surprise her with it when she had been extra good in all departments the night before. Tracie wished it were Jody cooking instead of Gail and the thought almost took away her appetite. Tracie didn't want to put a damper on dinner, so they sat down and ate. Thanks to Sam, dinner was full of talking and questions as well as jokes about her classmates. After dinner and homework, Sam settled down to watch some television. Tracie let her watch television for an hour then tucked her in to bed.

"How's Jody?" Gail asked taking a sip of her drink as Tracie re-entered the living room. She handed Tracie her own glass.

"You're not going to believe this Gail, but the psych doctor says Jody has no memory of being married to a woman. She thinks she's straight. They're going to be meeting a couple times a week. But otherwise, no change."

"Are you serious? She thinks she's straight."

"Gail, do I sound like I'm joking?"

"Wow, Tracie that's crazy. You gotta be patient; she'll get back to her gay self. It's just going to take time."

"I hope you're right."

They each took a seat on the couch. "She doesn't talk to us or anything. I asked her if she remembered Sam and she just gave me a blank expression." Tracie took a big swallow of her drink. The alcohol burnt going down, and it felt good knowing she could still feel something. She faced her sister and saw the worried look on her face.

"How was your day?"

Gail tucked her feet beneath her and sighed. "That bastard is really pushing it. Now, he says that because I didn't work, I shouldn't be entitled to the amount stated in the pre-nup. He is challenging the pre-nup, says he was too drunk to realize how much he was giving me."

"Gail what does the pre-nup say?" Tracie curiously asked.

"It says that Richard keeps everything that was acquired before we were married, and Richard will pay me ten thousand dollars a month to keep the lifestyle I'm accustomed to. This brownstone house would be mine under the agreement. If I can't afford it then the house would be sold, and we would split the proceeds. It also says I get a car and use of the vacation condo in Florida."

Tracie understood now why Richard wanted out of the prenup. She analyzed their relationship in her mind.

Gail had always been the dutiful wife while he was the master of the house. Tracie had often tried to tell Gail to go to school or volunteer with some charities, but Gail had felt that being a CEO's wife was a fulltime job. She didn't know how Gail had put up with Richard for the last ten years. Tracie had stopped liking him when she heard rumors that he was sleeping around, and that had been nine years ago.

"Wow," was all Tracie could say.

Gail's face took on a hard look. "I never thought he'd leave me. I did everything for him including ironing his funky drawers. How could that bastard bring his dirt to our home? He just thinks I should roll over and play dead like I did for the last ten years. Well, I'm not. Hell, yes, I want to contest the pre-nup. What I'm getting is just pocket change for him. With all I did I should be getting a lot more. I want him to know I'm not someone he can run over anymore. I want him to know I can fight and will fight when I have to."

"Hold up, Gail. You mean you're doing all this out of spite and greed?" Tracie asked, not believing her sister had it in her to be vengeful.

"Why not? I loved him and this is what he does," Gail said between sobs.

Tracie reached over and held her, trying to quiet her tears. "Gail, please think before you continue this game with him. Someone could get hurt. That's a pretty generous pre-nup and I don't think him contesting it will go anywhere."

Just as she was going to offer more sisterly advice, Sam came in. She looked from Tracie to Gail with a concerned look on her face.

"Everything okay?" she asked in a soft voice.

"Come here Sam. Everything's fine. Auntie Gail was laughing so hard at a joke on television she started to cry."

"Ooooh," Sam said.

"Let's have a family hug," Tracie said to them spreading her arms.

They all embraced. Then Tracie and Gail turned toward Sam and tickled her. They wanted to lighten the mood before Sam went back to sleep. Tracie and Gail walked Sam to her room and tucked her into bed.

"Goodnight, kiddo," Gail said as she kissed Sam on the cheek. "Night, Auntie Gail," Sam said blowing her a kiss.

"Sweet dreams and goodnight," Tracie said.

"Night mommy," Sam said as she turned over to cuddle her teddy bear.

# Jody's Visitors

When Tracie got to Jody's hospital door, she could hear voices inside. She pushed the door open and was surprised to see Jody's co-workers. "Hey," she said as she entered. The people in the room were all laughing with Jody. Tracie had met some of them at the few get togethers she had attended with Jody. Jody had never hidden their relationship, but she didn't broadcast her sexuality either.

Tracie was hurt that Jody seemed to enjoy their company more than hers. There was one man she didn't know standing by Jody's bed. He was introduced to her as Shawn Michaels. Tracie didn't particularly like the way he looked at Jody, and she definitely didn't like the way Jody seemed to be hanging on to his every word. There was more small talk before they gathered their things to leave. Tracie felt she should be the one getting Jody's attention, not some guy from work. Tracie didn't object, but Jody seemed sad to see them go.

Tracie's tone didn't hide her feelings. "Well, it seems you had no problem remembering them." She sank heavily into a stiff chair.

She held back the tears threatening to fall.

"They said someone called the office and told them that I'd been in an accident. Them being concerned co-workers, they came to see if everything was alright." Jody sipped some water, not knowing what else to say. "From what they said we all worked at the same law firm... and some of that I can vaguely remember."

"Who's Shawn Michaels?"

"He introduced himself and said he was a litigator. I don't remember him."

Tracie let it go. "Here are some more pictures for you and some of your favorite music." She set them on the table next to the bed. "Your mother wanted to be here but she's under doctor's orders to take it easy. Knowing your mother, she'll be here tomorrow never mind what the doctor says."

There was a silence while Tracie busied herself fanning out the photos. "There's a bunch of pictures of you, me and Sam on vacation. We took her to Disney World last summer."

Jody looked at the pictures. "I'm so sorry, but I just don't remember any of this."

Tracie watched helplessly.

"Jody, don't you remember anything about our relationship?" Tracie said, frustrated. She knew what she'd agreed to with Dr. Stable, but she couldn't help it. She wanted Jody back now. Dr. Stable could do things her way, and Tracie was going to do things *her* way.

Jody's face got very serious, and she sat up straight in the bed. She stared straight at Tracie. Her facial expression let Tracie know she was trying to remember.

"I'm scared, not knowing what my life was like. I'm trying. Please, as a friend, I hope you will help me," Jody said with tears falling.

Tracie just sat there not knowing what to say. She reached out and slowly placed her hand over Jody's to comfort her.

Jody let Tracie's hand rest a minute then put her own back under the cover.

"Are you okay?" Tracie asked

Jody just nodded yes. "I'm getting tired from all the company."

"Jody, I am your friend I've always been your friend but. I won't let you not remember us," she said defiantly.

Jody looked at Tracie and softly said, "I will be leaving here by the end of the week. I'll be going home with Ms. Jones."

Tracie sat stunned. Her throat burned. She wanted to cry, but more than that she wanted to scream. She knew what she'd agreed to with Dr. Stable, but this was going too far. "Don't you want to come home to me and Sam?"

Jody felt bad. "I just feel you want more than I can give you. You overwhelm me, talking of a child and relationship. I need time to process all that's going on and I feel Ms. Jones's would be better."

"You don't want to come home? How can things go back to being normal if you're not with us?" Tracie asked desperately.

Jody's face softened in thought. "By taking one day at time."

Tracie didn't know what else to say. She felt as if she was losing the love of her life. And Sam was losing her mother. Her heart was breaking but she was powerless in this situation. Right now, she knew that she had to do what Jody wanted because the thought of losing her was devastating.

"Thank you for the pictures; I'm sure that I'll remember something when I go through them," Jody interrupted her thoughts.

"You want to look at some now?" Tracie asked eagerly.

"No, it's getting late and visiting hours will be over soon."

"How about we look at them until they throw me out," Tracie smiled, hoping to lighten the mood. "Anyway, how are you going to know what you're looking at if I leave?"

"Tracie, not tonight. I need some time alone and I'm very tired. All of this is overwhelming."

Tracie could tell she was getting aggravated, so she thought it best to leave. "Okay." She stood and asked, "Would it be ok if I came by tomorrow?"

Jody shrugged. "Sure, that would be fine." Jody was exhausted. She gathered the pictures and stuck them in a drawer. She fell asleep to faces floating in her memory.

Tracie couldn't wait to call Ms. Jones. She walked briskly through the hall, dodging nurses and patients with I.V. poles. She pushed through the swinging doors to the waiting room.

She dialed the phone with a shaky hand. When she reached Ms. Jones, she wasted no time in getting to her point.

"Ms. Jones, why didn't you tell me that Jody is going home with you at the end of the week?"

"Tracie, I was just as surprised as you are when Dr Stable called me about Jody coming here. She said Jody made the decision on her own.

I thought it was best she tell you. Tracie, we both want what's best for Jody. I feel right now is not the time to bring up your relationship or even Sam. Dr. Stable feels she needs space and time. I don't feel you can give her that. I love Sam as much as any grandmother can, but right now it could be too much for Jody. Try and understand."

Tracie felt defeated and wondered, was this another way for Ms. Jones to keep them apart. "When will it be a good time to bring us up?"

"Let's give her some time," Ms. Jones said."

That was not what Tracie wanted to hear. She felt like she was being pushed to the side.

"Okay fine." She hung up the phone boiling inside.

# Loneliness

After she left the hospital, Tracie went straight to the liquor store. She figured if she were drunk,

she wouldn't and couldn't feel the pain. Two shots of tequila and her pain would indeed start to dull.

Her life was falling apart, and she wanted to be alone tonight. She knew Gail was out and going to pick up Sam from school. She left a message on the answering machine telling them she loved them and that she would be staying at the hospital. She knew they both would have questions, but she could deal with that tomorrow.

When she reached her apartment, she walked up the stairs slowly. She opened the door to quietness. She stood in the middle of the living room and cried. She poured two shots in a glass; the burning going down let her know she could still feel. Tracie sat in the nearest chair closest to the answering machine and pushed play. Her job had called for an update. She didn't bother calling back.

Needing to feel close to Jody, she walked toward her chair hit play on the CD player. Luther Vandross's "A House is Not a Home" filled the room.

The drink didn't take long to have the effect she was looking for. She started to feel tipsy. Jody's chair seemed out of reach, so she made a left to the bedroom where she collapsed on the bed and held tight to Jody's pillow. With tears in her eyes, she fell asleep. The next morning, she could hear the telephone ringing somewhere in the house. She knew she should answer it, but her body wouldn't let her move. She just wanted to lay there and remember every detail of Jody: her smell, her touch, and her skin. And then the thoughts turned horrific. What if she never comes back? What if she never remembers? What if she never accepts Sam? The phone kept ringing. She rushed to it this time suddenly panicked that it could be about Jody or Sam.

Her voice was rough from the night before. "Hello," the word rushed from her mouth.

"Tracie? Are you alright?" Gail asked.

"Yeah, I had a few drinks. Is Sam, okay?"

"Sam's fine. I just dropped her off at school. Do you want me to come over?"

"No, no I'm good. I'll be over later. How was everything last night? I'm really sorry I didn't make it over, but I just needed to be alone," Tracie said, still groggy.

"I understand. We ate, played dress up and watched television until bedtime. Of course, Sam asked for you. I told her you wanted to stay with Jody for the night. She was okay with that." "Gail, thanks for everything. I don't know what I would do without you."

"Hey, that's what sisters do."

"Anything new on the divorce?"

"No, not really. How's Jody?"

Tracie's voice grew sad. "I went to see her yesterday and there were people from her job there."

"Ms. Jones had to call her job to let them know what happened to her. Quite naturally her co-workers would want to go and see her." said Gail

"Yeah, I know but there was this guy that had Jody hanging on to his every word. I didn't like the whole scene. I questioned her about him, and she was fucking rude to me. Gail, I feel like I don't know her." Her voice trembled.

"Trace, you have to remember that right now you don't know her, and she doesn't know you. You have to hang in there. It will be okay. I'm you sister, I wouldn't lie to you."

Tracie didn't want to hear it. Not right now. All she knew was that she hurt. "I'll pick up Sam from the bus after school."

"Okay, I'll make a real meal for us."

"I won't be eating much, but Sam could use the veggies I'm sure," Tracie said. "Okay, see you later."

Tracie reluctantly opened the blinds to see what kind of day she was facing. Jody liked heavy drapes so when they made love it was always night. She stood at the window and looked at the people below and wondered what their lives were like. She had procrastinated long enough. It was time to go see Jody.

Like a woman on a mission, she walked through the hospital waiting room and pushed through the swinging doors to the madness of orderlies trying to get breakfast served to their patients.

Tracie knocked on Jody's door but didn't wait for a reply before walking in. "Hey, how you doing today?"

"Okay," Jody said flipping through the channels.

"How are your sessions going?" Tracie asked, trying to make conversation.

"Fine." Jody replied, still flipping the channels.

"Did you have breakfast? I see the carts in the hall are half full."

"Yes, all done."

Tracie cleared her throat not sure where to go from there. She decided to change the subject.

"Any visitors?" Tracie wanted to find out if Shawn in particular had been by.

Jody looked up from her magazine. "Why?"

"Just curious," Tracie said. "Did you look at the pictures?"

"Yes, I didn't remember anything. We seemed to have had a good time."

"Doesn't that tell you something about our relationship?"

"Yes, it tells me that we must have been good friends, that's all. I'm sorry if you were hoping for something else."

Hurt, Tracie softly said, "Okay. I'll check on you later." She headed into the hall and almost bumped into a nurse. She didn't see any of the chaos around her; she just wanted to breathe some air. She got in her car leaned back on the headrest and tears trickled down her face. She put the car in drive turned the music low and drove off. She drove around for hours going no place in particular. She was mad at herself for letting her emotions get the best of her. Jody had always held the strings to her heart. Her life was out of control and there was nothing she could do. When she looked down, her car was almost on empty, and it was time to pick up Sam. She stopped for gas and drove to the bus stop, pulling up just as the bus arrived at the corner. She waited until she saw Sam get off the bus before getting out of the car. She put on a cheerful smile.

"Sam," she called.

"Mommy, mommy," Sam said as she ran to her at full pace.

"Hey, Sunshine." She gave Sam a big hug, her forced smile turning real.

"Are we going home?" Sam asked.

"No, not yet but soon," Tracie said. "Don't you like it at Auntie Gail's?" "Yeah, but I miss my bed," Sam said in a whiny voice.

"We'll be going home soon," Tracie said again. "Tell me what you did in school today."

"I diiid math, reading and played a game."

Tracie laughed. "Played a game? I wish I went to school with you." "Oh, mommy," Sam said laughing.

She chatted away all the way to Gail's. Tracie was happy not to have to think about Jody for a minute.

"Hey sis?" Tracie shouted as they entered the house.

"Hey Auntie Gail?" Sam shouted as she ran to the kitchen to see if Gail was in there.

"Hey, you," Gail said as she scooped up Sam to give her a big kiss.

"Mmmm, I smell something," Sam said as she wrinkled her nose.

"Broccoli." Gail laughed at her niece's reaction.

"I don't like broccoli," Sam said whining.

"You have to eat a little," Tracie said.

"How are you doing?" Gail asked Tracie.

Tracie looked over at Sam. "Why don't you go and wash up for dinner and use soap." "Ooookay," Sam said obviously disappointed that she had to leave the conversation.

"It hurts so much, Gail, not to be able to reach her."

"I know, but this is a situation that you are going to have to be patient with," Gail said.

"I have to try harder."

Gail gave her some sisterly advice. "No, Trace, you have to try and reach her by being a friend first."

Tracie was about to cry. She heard Sam coming so she turned her head so Sam couldn't see her face.

"What's wrong with mommy?" Sam asked coming back into the room.

"She's okay but some broccoli juice got into her eye."

"I don't like broccoli even more now," Sam said making a face.

"Okay, young lady to the table you will go," Gail told her.

Sam sat down at the table and Gail fixed three plates. Tracie hardly ate; Sam pushed the broccoli around her plate and Gail ate slowly. After dinner they played Scrabble and got ready for bed. It had been a long day, and everybody was tired. Tracie tossed and turned but eventually she fell asleep.

# SEPTEMBER 2016

65

# Jody Going Home

Jody had been in the hospital two weeks. All her bruises were healed and it was time to leave. She stepped outside the hospital ward's swinging doors into the waiting room. There was a man holding a sign with her name on it: Jody Jones.

She approached him. "Do I know you?"

"If you're Jody Jones I'm here to take you home."

"Who sent you?" She was unsure of really what to do since she didn't recognize him. Just as Jody was going to send the man away Dr. Stable walked up.

"Jody, its ok. Ms. Jones just called to let me know that there would be a car service here to take you home. I'm sorry I didn't get down here sooner to clear up any misunderstanding."

"No misunderstanding. Everything is good. If you're ready, we can be on our way," the driver said to them both.

"Sure, why not?" Jody said as she started following the man. She was scared, anxious and excited at what lay beyond the waiting room doors. All she knew was there was a world outside that she almost had no recognition of. She was so wrapped up in her thoughts she didn't say goodbye to Dr. Stable but left her standing in the waiting room.

As she rode, a feeling of dread came over her at the thought of living with a woman she didn't even remember. A woman she was told was her mother.

She looked out the cab window hoping for any sign of her lost memory, but there was none. The houses she saw were neat with little patches of grass just big enough for a small barbeque in the summer. She could catch glimpses of swimming pools in the back of some of the houses. There were small children riding bicycles and big boys playing basketball without shirts. The trees were full of leaves and little flowers of different colors. It seemed that the man wanted her to take this all in because he stopped for lights at every corner.

The cab stopped in front of one of those neat houses. Only, this one had a big sign with the words "Welcome Home Jody" across the porch.

"Here we are," said the man.

Jody felt scared, not knowing what she would find beyond the front door.

She sat and pretended not to hear him.

The man cleared his throat. "Ms Jones, you're home."

"What? Oh, we're here?"

"Yes, no charge. Your mother took care of everything up front," he said.

"Okay," Jody said as she opened the door.

She walked up the four cement stairs and knocked on the door. No answer. She knocked again but harder. She heard a distant voice holler for her to come in. She cracked open the door and pushed slowly.

"SURPRISE!"

She was taken aback at the swarm of people. They came from everywhere, seemingly from the walls themselves. Face after face came at her. She recognized no one. She moved her eyes feverishly around them, looking for Ms. Jones. She was relieved when she saw her. She moved timidly in her direction.

Ms. Jones saw the frightened look on her face and moved quickly to meet her.

"Jody, honey, I invited some family and friends over to welcome you home. They all wanted to come see you at the hospital, but the doctor didn't think it was a good idea. I hope you don't mind. You got a lot of people that love you."

She ushered Jody in and started the introductions.

"This is your Aunt Beverly, your cousins Jamal and Nicole, your Uncle Paul. The two young ladies over there are your best friends Charisse and Dee.

Jody's heart raced. People stared with smiles. She looked to her mother.

"Ms. Jo—, I don't know what to call you. I mean mom isn't appropriate and Ms. Jones seems too formal. I appreciate you having these people over, but you shouldn't have. I don't…I don't know any of them.

"Why don't you call me by my first name?" Ms. Jones said. "I'm Diane. They just wanted to say hello. I told them that they couldn't stay long." She said the last bit very loudly so everyone could hear. She took Jody's hand and started to move toward the kitchen.

One of the women that Diane said was her best friend walked up to her.

"Hey girl. How you doing? It's good to have you home.

Jody looked at her, not sure what to make of her with the rings in her nose and a skirt that a seven-year-old could wear.

The other woman, Dee, said to her. "Where is Tracie anyway?"

"I have no idea?" Jody said not understanding why she was asking her about Tracie."Calm down. She didn't mean no harm," said Charisse.

"I'm tired." Jody said.

"Okay girl," Charisse said. "I just thought you might want to go to a club after being in the

hospital."

Jody looked at her with fire in her eyes. She couldn't believe these were the type of people she socialized with.

Diane realized a party was idea bad. She asked everyone to leave. "I'm sorry if this was too much for you," Diane said softly after they had gone.

"It's been a long day and I'm tired," Jody said.

"Are you hungry?" Diane said as they were passing the kitchen to Jody's bedroom.

"A piece of whatever smells so good would be nice," Jody said wetting her lips.

"You always loved my fried chicken," Diane said as she smiled. "Glad to see that hasn't changed. You always liked a leg and thigh. How about that and a biscuit?"

Jody smiled. "That would be nice." She settled into the room while Diane made her a plate.

The powder blue room was fairly large. It had a full-size bed and a desk with computer. The curtains matched the bedspread in color. There was a walk-in closet full of shoes and clothes, hanging from end to end in the closet. A wall unit held a 42-inch flat screen television along with a DVD player. Jody walked around touching everything, trying to spark something in her brain. Diane brought the chicken and biscuits in, and Jody settled in for a night of television. They agreed to talk more in the morning.

Jody slept like a baby that night. The bed felt like it was made for her; it enveloped her body in a warm cocoon. She slept until nine the next morning when Diane knocked on the door with a tray filled with assorted pastries and coffee. Yummy.

"I thought you might like this," Diane said. "These were your favorite breakfast sweets along with black coffee."

"Thank you."

They spent the day looking at pictures hoping something would jar her memory. When it came to a picture of Jody at five years old holding a raggedy teddy bear Diane stopped

"You see that teddy bear? We tried everything to get you to part with it. We even took you to the store to get a replacement, but you refused to let that one go. It only had one ear, one foot and the stuffing kept coming out. I'd sew it but it would keep unraveling You were stubborn when you made up your mind about something that was it."

"What happened to that bear?" Jody asked.

"If you look in the top of your closet, you're find your one foot one ear bear in plastic."

"Wow, you mean you kept it all this time?"

"Yes, I did."

Jody was moved by Diane's gesture. "Tell me more."

"You were a daddy's girl. Your father spoiled you, I think to make up for moving around so much that you didn't have friends. He loved the military but hated the moving part. You were his everything from the time you were born until he closed his eyes. He loved you very much. He would be so proud of everything you've accomplished. There was nothing to good for you. He didn't care what he had to do to make you happy. You were his star and he made sure everyone knew it.

Tracie called a few times during the day interrupting them, but Jody asked Diane to tell her she was busy. Diane continued after each interruption to tell Jody of her childhood. Diane wanted to make sure Jody understood that they loved her to death, and how devastating it was when her father died of prostate cancer. She told Jody that she didn't have a boyfriend until she was eighteen and then there was a steady stream. Nobody serious but from what Jody would tell her, it was just young people having fun.

The phone rang again. "Hello," Diane said answering the phone. She whispered to Jody that it was Tracie.

"Hello again, Ms. Jones," Tracie said on the other end.

Jody shook her head no. "Tracie, I told you earlier that Jody is busy. Give her some time to get settled. Please give her some space." Diane hung up the phone annoyed with Tracie's calls.

***

Jody's first venture would be going to a meeting with Dr. Stable at the hospital. She would have been out the hospital only a few days. Jody was anxious to get started. The day before her doctor's visit, she told Diane she was going to take public transportation to get there. She wanted to do things on her own. Diane was hesitant but couldn't stop her. She felt like Jody was six and taking the bus to school for the first time.

"You got everything?" Diane anxiously asked.

"Yes, Diane. I'll be fine."

Things had been going well so far. Diane was doing a lot of talking and Jody seemed to be taking it all in.

"You got the number to call me if you get lost?" Diane asked.

"Yep," Jody said as she opened the front door and a cool morning wind hit her in the face. When the bus arrived, she took a seat and stared out the window at the bustle of city life. There were people dressed for work and kids with schoolbooks dressed in uniforms. There was a man with a shopping cart full of what appeared to be junk, yelling to anyone that would listen.

*Wow*, Jody thought. *This was my life.* She arrived at the hospital and went straight to Dr. Stable's office. The receptionist recognized her from previous visits.

"Hello, Ms. Jones. Dr. Stable said to send you right in."

Dr. Stable took off her wire framed glasses and stood when Jody came in.

"Well, how's it feel to be home?" Dr. Stable asked.

"Okay."

"How'd you feel to be called Ms. Jones by Maria?"

"What...I guess I wasn't paying attention to what she called me."

"Well how does it feel to know your last name is Jones?" Dr. Stable asked.

Jody gave it some thought and finally said. "I guess it feels ok."

Dr. Stable thought it best to move on in the session. "Jody, as I've told you this is a very unusual case of selective memory loss. Your memory is sort of abstract. I mean it's all over the place with nothing to join the pieces together. It's like putting together a puzzle with small and big pieces; however, the small pieces of your memory are hidden. I think it would benefit you to start a journal that you keep with you at all times. That way when you think you remember something you can write it down right away before you forget. When you come for your next visit, we can discuss what you've written and see if we can add to that thought.

Dr. Stable had gotten family history and pictures from Ms. Jones. They talked about her upbringing and religion. She and Jody practiced some memory retrieval techniques for an hour. The time was up, and Dr. Stable reminded her to write down anything that she thought could relate to her prior life.

She walked through the empty receptionist office out into the bright sunshine. She had a few minutes to walk two blocks for the bus back to Diane's. She took her time. As Jody rode home, she decided she was ready to explore her new world. She was ready to go back to work. As soon as she arrived home, she told Diane.

"I know you're anxious to know what your life was like but are you sure you're ready to go back to work?" Diane asked.

"Yep," Jody said with butterflies in her stomach.

"What did Dr. Stable say about this?"

"I didn't tell her," Jody said looking at her straight in the eye.

"Well, how do you know you're ready?" Diane returned Jody's eye contact. "I mean how do you know this won't set back any progress you've made?"

Jody was getting annoyed. "I'm going to work tomorrow or the next day. One way or another I'm going."

Diane felt Jody was moving a little too fast. She decided to call Jody's job to see if they could stall her coming back. She had been taken aback at the tone that Jody used with her. "I'll make the call to talk to your boss. I want to make sure they're ready to have you back."

When she came back from the den where the phone was Jody was back in her room looking at outfits.

"I spoke with your boss, Mr. Kincaid, and he wants to make sure everything is in place. He said give him a few days."

"What does he mean everything is in place?"

"I would imagine he has to get someone to help you catch up.""That's fine," Jody said as she stretched out on her bed for a nap.

Diane quietly closed the door behind her.

# Gail's Lunch
## With Richard

Richard called Gail for a meeting without their lawyer. Gail couldn't imagine what he would want after all this time. She was skeptical but at the same time intrigued. They met at an out of the way restaurant in Manhattan.

She didn't mention it to Tracie because she knew Tracie would say she was stupid to go. Gail got dressed after Tracie took Sam to the bus. She didn't know why she cared how she looked but she kept switching outfits, not satisfied with any of them. She looked at herself in the mirror and thought nice body. A verrry nice body that Richard will never have again. She thought of Richard's bitch coming to her house and the way he left her. She threw on a pair of jeans and a sweater. When she arrived at the restaurant, Richard was already seated and dressed in a suit and tie.

"You didn't go to much trouble getting ready," Richard said sarcastically.

"Why should I?" Gail responded just as sarcastically. "What do you want Richard?"

"I thought that maybe we could come to some kind of agreement between us without the suits," Richard said while gesturing for the waiter. "What will you have?"

"Water. Thank you."

"Another scotch and water for me," Richard said.

"That's new," Gail said smartly.

"What, the suit?"

"No, drinking so early."

"Yeah, I know." Richard looked down at his drink and spoke. "Gail, I know it's not your concern, but I've lost some big accounts recently and...."

"What has that got to do with me?" Gail said cutting him off.

"Well, I was hoping that we could come to some reasonable decision concerning my assets." He looked at Gail with his baby blues.

"Don't try it, Richard. I'm not falling for that pitiful act of yours. What do you want me to agree to? Throwing out the pre-nup." She dug for her keys to leave.

Richard, obviously sensing that this conversation was not going his way, tried another tactic.

"Gail, you know there's not a day that goes by that I don't wish we could start over again. I mean you were a good wife to me." He reached out his hand.

"Save the bullshit Richard," Gail said. "It's over, we're done. I don't know what you hoped to accomplish by this meeting. I want exactly what you promised me, nothing less, and more if I can get it." She grabbed her purse and nearly ran out of the restaurant, leaving Richard sitting there nursing his drink.

# Tracie Back To Work

When Tracie got to work, she went straight to the principal's office to find out what's been happening.

"Welcome back." The principal said

"It's good to be back. How's things here?"

"Not much, we hired a temp gym teacher Ms. Keenesha Jordan. She's waiting for her position at College of St. Francis Xavier. She is highly qualified with a master's degree in physical education. She has glowing marks from her last principal.

"Cool. Let me get down there."

When Tracie got to the door the kids were playing basketball. The temp gym teacher was on the sideline. Tracie didn't enter right away. For some reason she was transfixed by the caramel skinned, short, dreadlocked gym teacher. She was feminine in appearance but yet there was something aggressive in her movements. After a few minutes, the gym teacher must have sensed someone looking at her because she turned toward the closed door. She started to walked in Tracie's direction. Tracie opened the door, and the kids came running toward her.

"Ms. Davis, Ms. Davis!" the kids yelled while trying to get a hug from her.

"Well, you're Ms. Davis?" Ms. Jordan said loudly as she approached the loud group. "And you must be Ms. Jordan," Tracie said yelling over the children. "It's nice to meet you. I heard some good things about you from the principal."

Ms. Jordan seemed to sense that the kids were getting out of hand, so she blew her whistle for them to line up.

"Okay, kids, give Ms. Davis a chance to breathe. You can all talk to her after I've caught her up on what we've been doing. Please continue with your basketball game." She turned to Tracie. "Ms. Davis why don't we go into our office for some coffee?"

"That sounds good to me," Tracie said as she followed her to their office where she sat on the little couch.

"It's nice to have you back. I heard you had a family emergency," Ms. Jordan said as she handed Tracie her coffee.

"Mmmm, just like I like it," Tracie said looking at the coffee.

"I hope everything is going well," Ms. Jordan said with noticeable compassion.

"Everything is good. Thanks for asking."

There was silence for a while as if they both were waiting for the other to speak.

"Well, what's been going on here?" Tracie asked.

Ms. Jordan went over to the bulletin board and as she handed Tracie the schedule their hands touched for just a moment. The electricity made Tracie jerk her hand back and drop her end of the paper. Tracie felt the need to say something. "I'm sorry, I thought I had it." "No, need to be sorry. Here," Ms. Jordan said handing the paper to Tracie again. This time Tracie made sure not to let their hands touch.

"Well, partner, it looks like we have our work cut out for us this semester."

"Mmm, yeah." Ms. Jordan said sipping her coffee. "Here comes out first class. We better get out there." It was a full morning of basketball and kids screaming.

The time went by fast and before they knew it the lunch bell was ringing.

"Well, it's getting late, and I need to pick up my little monster from the bus. It's a half a day for her and we need to do some bonding," Tracie said.

"I heard you had a little one. I don't have any children, but my sister's kids are always over. I better get out there. I can't leave them alone for very long—no telling who will end up on the floor."

They both laughed as they started for the door.

See you tomorrow?" Ms. Jordan asked.

"You bet," Tracie said and walked across the gym floor.

# An Unexpected Meeting

"Mommy, mommy," Sam said as she ran toward Tracie from the school bus.

"How's my girl?" Tracie asked with a big smile on her face.

"Good," Sam said grinning back. "Is mommy Jody ready to come home yet?"

Tracie knelt. "Well, mommy Jody had to go home to Grandma's house. Since I'm at work and you're at school the doctor felt it best that she stay with Grandma."

"I don't mind missing school to be with Mommy," Sam said sadly.

"I know, honey, but mommy Jody wouldn't want you to and plus Grandma is home all day with no company."

"Can we go visit her?" Sam said with excitement in her voice.

"The doctor feels she needs to be a little stronger before she can have visitors."

"I miss her," Sam said with tears in her eyes.

"Hey, she misses you too. Don't cry, you know mommy Jody wouldn't want you to be sad. Turn that frown upside down," Tracie said trying to lighten the mood. "How about we go get some lunch?"

"Yaaay, McDonald's," Sam said knowing that this would lead to a game because Tracie hated McDonald's.

"How about Wendy's?" Tracie said.

"Nope, McDonald's," Sam said.

"Why?" Tracie asked.

"All beef burger with special sauce annnnd," Sam said forgetting the rest.

"And?"

"I can't remember the rest," Sam whined.

"Okay, here's what we'll do. If you can guess the number, I'm thinking we'll go to McDonald's."

Sam put on her thinking face and said, "Seven," sheepishly.

"No, but I'll give you one more chance."

Sam really went into deep thought and her forehead wrinkled. "One," she said with all the confidence she could muster.

"You're right. I guess it's McDonald's," Tracie said smiling.

"Yay," Sam said jumping up down.

***

The evening at Gail's went as it usually did, with Tracie helping Sam with her homework and watching television before her bedtime.

It had been a few days since Tracie had called Jody and after the earlier conversation with Sam, she felt the need to hear her voice.

"Hello," Ms. Jones said answering the phone.

"Ms. Jones, its Tracie. May I speak with Jody?"

Ms. Jones didn't attempt at conversation. Tracie heard her shuffling her feet as she moved away from the phone. Then the feet came back.

"Tracie, she said she's busy."

"How's she doing?" Tracie asked.

"She's doing good. She's been going to her sessions and she's going back to work soon," Ms. Jones said.

"Do you think she's ready?" Tracie asked.

"No, I think it's too soon, but you know Jody. She can be stubborn" Ms. Jones said.

"Yeah, I know. Have you talked with the doctor?" Tracie asked, trying to sound gentle.

"No, I haven't, but I did talk with her boss to see if he'd delay her coming back to work."

"That's good at least; that's something to slow her down. Please tell her I called, and I'll call before the week is out."

The separation was killing her inside, but she didn't want to lose Jody completely by doing anything that would upset her. The praying she did every night didn't seem to be helping. This nightmare didn't seem to be ending anytime soon.

Gail walked into the room. "Hey, girl, what's up?"

"Nothing. I called to talk to Jody, but she's still not talking to me."

Gail tried to sound upbeat. "I know it's hard, but give her time. One day you'll both look back on this and laugh."

"I hope you're right," Tracie said. She changed the subject quickly so she wouldn't think about the telephone call anymore. "I got a temp to help with the kids in gym."

"How'd he/she seem?" Gail asked.

"She seemed nice, and the kids seem to like her." Tracie smiled a little, unable not to. It felt good.

Gail squinted. "Is that a little smile I see?"

"No," Tracie hurriedly said. "I mean... yes. And I feel guilty as hell now thanks. I meet someone new and talk to her for an hour and suddenly I'm smiling. Not to mention that my spouse has no memory of me, our daughter, or our life together. I have no right to be smiling."

"It's just a smile. And you deserve a smile. You're right. Your life is hell." Gail laughed."I'm going to bed." Tracie said, annoyed at her reaction.

"Me too," Gail said. "Try not to be so hard on yourself."

The next day, Tracie dropped Sam at the bus while Gail slept in. She stopped at Starbucks for coffee and the morning paper. As she sat down to read, her mind drifted to the morning snuggle sessions with Jody. She was brought back to life by Ms. Jordan clearing her throat. She had a cup of coffee in her hand.

"Hey, I've been standing here for hours," Ms. Jordan said grinning.

"You have not because I haven't been here for hours," Tracie said smiling going along with the joke.

"It's getting late. If we don't want a riot in gym we better be on our way. Let's walk and talk," Ms. Jordan said. "And by the way, Ms. Jordan sounds like you're talking to my mother.

Call me Kee."

"I think it's best if we remain professional in school, so Ms. Jordan would be better," Tracie said.

"You're right. I forget that I'm not at the high school level anymore where things are more relaxed."

"What are you doing with us low level gym teachers anyway?" Tracie asked as they left Starbucks.

"I'm just waiting for my position at College of St Francis Xavier."

"Well, we're glad to have you," Tracie said with a smile.

"Could you check the schedule to make sure there weren't any changes made for today?" Tracie asked when they'd reached their office. "Sometimes they sneak in the office with a revised one."

Ms. Jordan looked at the schedule. "We've got a full day with no changes: three fifth grade classes have sixty minutes each of gym in the morning. The afternoon is a repeat just with the six graders."

"Cool, let's get started," Tracie said.

They were both busy with work but every now and then Tracie felt liked she was being watched. Every time she was near Ms. Jordan, she felt her clit jump. She decided it best to keep her distance. Tracie was glad when the bell rang to go home.

***

Sam was home by the time Tracie arrived. "Mommy, look what I did," Sam said proudly. Tracie picked up the picture Sam had drawn. She didn't have a clue of what it was. "Very nice."

"Do you know what it is?" Sam asked.

"Of course, it's a chicken," Tracie said smiling.

"Nooo," Sam said.

"Okay, one more guess. Is it a turtle?" Tracie asked looking at Gail for help.

"Mommy, it's a bird sleeping," Sam said.

"Well, it's a very nice bird sleeping," Tracie said bending down to kiss her.

"Let's get ready for dinner," Gail said.

They had dinner and watched television. Tracie read Sam a bedtime story. She was beat herself and decided to turn in, with thoughts of Jody on her mind. She knew Jody was going back to work. The thought brought about images of the guy from the hospital Shawn. She tossed and turned for hours before drifting off to sleep.

# OCTOBER 2016

# Jody Back To Work

The day had finally come for Jody to return to work; it had been a month since Diane had spoken to her boss. She got up early and was too excited to eat. She dressed in a cream-colored suit with dark brown heels—she'd tried on several different outfits before settling on this one. When ready, she went across the street and caught the bus, the same bus she had been taking to see Dr. Stable.

***

Jody found the building from the address Diane had written on a piece of paper. Looking up at it, she was quite impressed. The building was tall and all glass.

She stepped into the revolving doors and came out inside a marble lobby with a guard desk over to the side. She walked to it and gave the guard her name, then he instructed her to take the elevator to the twenty-fifth floor. When she arrived on the floor, there was a bustle of people walking quickly with papers in their hands. She walked over to a desk in the front with a sign that said receptionist. The receptionist recognized her and walked her down to her office. As they walked, people spoke to her. She politely spoke back. She didn't have a clue who they were, but the welcome felt good.

They arrived at a door with a name plate that said *Ms. Jody Jones*. The office was huge with a big wooden desk and two enormous windows. There was a couch and low table over to the side, along with some impressive artwork on the walls

The receptionist left her alone after showing her how to operate the phone. Jody sat behind her desk without a clue as to what to do next. She remembered what Diane said this morning about taking things slow.

There was a knock on the door interrupting her thought.

"Hey Jody, I'm your very own personal welcoming committee," Shawn said with a smile, standing in the doorway.

"Hey, Shawn, right," Jody said, not sure that she remembered his name correctly. "Yep, that's me." He was still smiling. He had his hand behind his back as he approached the desk. When he got closer, he whipped out a dozen roses.

"Wow, do you welcome everyone back to work like this?" she asked with a big smile.

"Nope, only the pretty ones," he said laughing. He looked nice. The brother definitely had it going on. Tall, dark, and handsome; any woman would love that butt of his. She knew she was blushing. Whew.

"Hey," he said. "Are you alright?"

"Yeah, I'm probably having one of those women's moments." She realized it wasn't a good answer for her blushing.

Shawn didn't seem to know how to respond. He cleared his throat. "How do you like being back?"

"So far, so good. I just got here."

"I don't want to rush you, but how about lunch?"

"Sounds good to me." They stared at each other for a long moment before he turned to leave.

She smiled, trying to hide her nervousness. He smiled as well and breezed through the door.

After sitting for a while, she started opening the desk drawers. She found some files and a picture of her, Sam and Tracie smiling. She put the picture back in the drawer, not wanting to deal with that at the moment.

She had started to read the files when there was a knock on the door.

"Come in," Jody said.

"Jody, I'm Mr. Carter. Your boss."

"It's nice to meet you. I sort of remember you," she said cheerfully.

"Well, that's good. Or maybe not so good, depending on how you feel about your boss." He chuckled.

"I think the memories are good," she said, laughing as well.

"I'm glad you still have your sense of humor."

"Thank you."

He nodded and sank his hands in his pockets. "Well, I just came by to let you know if you need anything, I'm here for you. Don't hesitate to ask."

"I hope you can help me with something right now. And believe me I feel so foolish asking this but exactly... what did I do?"

"You were, I mean are, an attorney. The cases you dealt with were mostly child custody," Mr. Carter explained. "You are a damn good attorney. Sort of a one-woman children's advocate." "Really?" She was surprised to hear how good her work was, but hearing it felt good.

"I thought we should have an impromptu meeting. Let me gather everyone," Mr. Carter said.

Mr. Carter returned with co-workers in tow. They all welcomed Jody back with hugs and kisses. They agreed that she wasn't ready for anything heavy or too intense. She would perform clerical duties like typing briefs, reading law books, and answering phones. It wasn't what she expected. She understood with her mind in a puzzle actually presenting someone in court might be a bit much. She was to begin working with Karen, another attorney, who had a case involving two women who adopted a little boy and were now breaking up. One of the women was a teacher accused of sleeping with an underage girl in her classroom during after school hourd.

"Wow, that's deep," Jody said as she read the brief.

"Yeah, women teachers are usually accused of sleeping with underage boys," Karen told her.

"This is something. I just can't believe it," Jody said with amazement.

"Being a lawyer, you hear and see it all. Be glad you can't remember a lot of the mess that happens out there," Karen said pointing out the window.

"Well, were do I start?" Jody asked.

"Why not read some law books on same sex adoption? It's your first day. Take it slow."

Jody had questions after reading the same sex brief and law books on the subject "I don't understand why you're representing someone accused of raping a child?" Jody asked.

"Because we were hired by the accused. She says she's innocent and that the girl is making it all up. She doesn't want this case to impact her chances of getting her son. Jody, as a lawyer, everyone is innocent until proven guilty."

"Wow, a kid would make something like that up?"

"Kids will do the darndest things sometimes. You just never know kids these days.

"My concern at this point is whether the accused will try to take the boy and run. This case has been getting a lot of negative publicity. The abuse case has to be taken care of first, before the parental case can

"Karen, how can I help? I know I have a lot to learn. I don't wanna be in the way but I'm anxious to get started."

"Let's keep it simple to start. You keep reading law books and doing the other clerical things that are needed. Jody, keep asking questions. It'll all come back. I'll keep you in the loop as much as I can." Karen said, trying not to hurt Jody's feelings.

Jody was deflated. It didn't sound like she was going to be doing anything important anytime soon. "Oh, I see."

"Jody, you were a damn good lawyer and one day soon you'll be damn good again," Karen said to her with confidence.

Jody didn't expect this, but what choice did she have? "Thanks, Karen, for saying that."

"No need." She patted Jody's shoulder as she left the office.

A few minutes later, there was another knock at the door. Shawn came in pushing a small table. The table had a single rose in a vase on a white silk tablecloth. He had two covered plates at opposite ends of the table.

"Is it lunch time already?" she asked.

"It is indeed." he said. "I thought it would be nice if we spend some time alone to get to know each other better," Shawn said showing his pearly whites.

He rolled the table in front of the big windows with a beautiful view of downtown. He placed two chairs in front of the covered plates then, like a maître d, he escorted her to a seat.

He uncovered the plates and she saw the biggest hamburgers she'd ever seen...as far as she knew.

The thick crispy fries where hidden by the enormous burger.

"I asked everyone what you liked to eat for lunch," he said. "I wanted to be sure I got your favorite."

She smiled. "Hamburgers." She wasn't sure if this was her favorite or not; she couldn't remember.

"Yep, hamburgers," he said. "Oh, I forget the Coke." He pulled two cans from his pocket.

"Shawn, this is nice. I really mean it." She glanced down at her plate. "And this burger is amazing."

"Then how about dinner tomorrow?" he asked as he reached for her hand.

"Sure," Jody said, not letting the burger go with either of her hands.

"Hey, I just wanted to hold your hand," Shawn said, sensing her reluctance.

"I know, but there's ketchup and mustard all over them," Jody said.

"I don't care. You don't have to be afraid. I won't try to keep your hand," Shawn said, smiling.

"I didn't think you would, but I prefer to keep my hand on the burger," Jody said. They ate and made idle chitchat.

"Okay, I got it, but tomorrow will be a different story," Shawn said.

"What do you mean? I hate surprises."

"You know, what I've realized is that people who say they hate surprises actually love surprises. They say they hate it, so you'll tell them. I'm not falling for it," Shawn said, laughing.

"Is that so?" Jody said, standing and walking over to the door. "Since you are so smart, and you know what people actually want then what do I actually want at this very minute?" Shawn stood and walked to the door. He put his hand on the doorknob. "Well since you walked to the door, I would guess lunch is over."

Jody took two steps back so she wouldn't be so close to him. "You *are* smart. See you later." Jody typed briefs, read law books, and answered phones for the rest of the day. When no one was looking she read the brief before typing. She was intrigued by some of the cases and was especially interested in the case Karen had. She couldn't wait to get more information on it. When she got home, Diane was waiting to hear about her day. Jody told Diane it was good day. She declined dinner because she just wanted to go to her room to unwind. She thought about Karen's case, lunch with Shawn, and then thought of the picture in her desk drawer. Why was that picture there, she wondered?

She snuggled under her covers and drifted off to sleep.

# A Date

The next morning, Tracie quietly went into the living room and called Jody. She had been on her mind all night, as usual.

"Hello," a groggy voice answered.

"Hi, Jody. It's Tracie."

"Do you know what time it is?" She sounded mad. Tracie had forgotten that unless it was sex, Jody was not a morning person

"Okay, you got me. I'm awake."

"How's everything going?" Tracie asked.

"Everything is going good."

"That's good. Are you still going to the therapy sessions with Dr. Stable?" "Yep, I'm still going," Jody said.

Tracie could tell she was getting impatient. "Well, when can I see you?"

"I'm not sure. I need more time to get used to everything," Jody said.

"Sure, I understand, but I'm going to keep asking until you say yes. You been doing anything else?"

"I have a date," Jody said with a little too much enthusiasm for Tracie.

"With whom?" Tracie felt anger and jealousy rising within her.

"Shawn, the guy from work.

"Oh, I see."

"Tracie can we talk later."

***

Tracie sat motionless, fighting the biting tears. She went into the kitchen to make coffee and start Sam's breakfast. She was hurt and angry all at the same time. Gail came in just as she sat down.

"Good morning," Gail said.

"What's so good about it?" She stared into her coffee.

"What's up with you?"

She took a deep breath "I called Jody this morning to see if we could get together, but that guy from her job beat me to it."

"Ouch. That's rough."

"Rough? I feel like I'm dying inside."

"You have to keep trying. Don't let her going out with him discourage you. If you want her back then you're going to have to fight for her," Gail said with conviction.

"Yeah, I know you're right but what gets me, Gail, is that she is my spouse and we had it good. Then some freak accident causes her to lose the most important part of her memory—me and Sam. What the fuck?"

"Yeah, this has been some year so far, you with Jody and me getting a divorce," Gail said.

"Has there been anything going on with that?"

"Richard is trying to turn the few friends that sided with me to his side by saying I'm a lesbian. Can you believe that?"

"How'd you find out what he was saying?" Tracie asked.

"Sheila told me. Her husband is Richard's tennis partner."

"Hey, don't sweat being a lesbian. It isn't bad. It's not like he said you murdered that bitch of his," Tracie said with a grin.

"You are so right."

Sam came in the kitchen rubbing her eyes.

"Mommy, Auntie Gail, I'm hungry. What's for breakfast?"

"Hey how about saying good morning first?" Tracie asked, embracing her with a tight hug.

"Sor-ry, Good morning. What's for breakfast?"

"How about bacon and French toast?" Tracie asked.

"Mmmmm."

"You go wash up and get dressed," Tracie said.

"Hey, Trace, I got this. You go and get ready for work. It gives me something to do besides thinking about how much I hate Richard," Gail said.

"Are you sure? I got time."

"Yeah, let me spoil my niece. I'll take her to the bus stop and pick her up this afternoon so you don't have to rush home," Gail said.

"What am I supposed to do? It's not like Jody wants to see me."

Gail put the bacon in the pan. "Go for a drink or walk. It will do you good."

# The Temp

Ms. Jordan was in the office drinking coffee when Tracie got to work.

"Hey," she said when she saw Tracie come through the door.

Tracie walked straight to the coffee pot. "Hey, what's going on?"

"You seem preoccupied," Ms. Jordan said.

"Yeah, maybe a little but it's okay. Has anything on the schedule changed for today?"

"Well, Ms. Davis, this is your lucky day. Today is an administrative day nothing to do but paperwork."

"Yeah, I forgot. I hate having to do paperwork."

"Yeah, I know what you mean," Ms. Jordan said

"Let's get started. Since I've been out, I don't really have any but let me help you with yours."

"I didn't want to ask, but I'm swamped," Ms. Jordan said, pulling out a stack of papers.

When Tracie saw the papers, her eyes widened. "You really hate paperwork."

They laughed while working all morning without a break. At lunch time Tracie went to the deli across the street for turkey sandwiches and unsweetened iced tea for both of them. Tracie was amazed that someone else liked their tea the same as her. Jody always turned up her nose and said yuck. They worked for a couple more hours after lunch, hardly making a dent in the mounds of paperwork. Then it was time to go home. They were both exhausted, but Tracie wasn't ready to go home. She needed to do something to keep her mind off of Jody.

"How about we go across the street to the bar for a drink?" Tracie asked while gathering her things.

"Sure, why not. I need to unwind," Ms. Jordan said while gathering her things as well.

They walked across the street to a bar that looked more like someone's house. Located in an

old brownstone building, the décor was amazing. Big-screen televisions were mounted on the walls. The floor and bar area were decorated in a dark wood. The back of the club had couches with low tables. The front had wooden tables with cushioned chairs. There was an old juke box in a corner, and a small area in the back where the band usually played.

They walked to the back where they could talk.

"Wow, this is nice," Ms. Jordan said, taking in the atmosphere.

"Yeah, let's sit over there by the window."

Tracie sat down. "This place is very deceptive from the outside."

"Yeah, you are so right. I looked at this place a thousand times and never would have guessed it was a club. I thought it was somebody's house."

"What should we talk about, Ms. Jordan?" Tracie asked, coming out of her daydream of wishing Jody were sitting across from her.

"First thing we're not in school now, how about you call me Kee, and I call you Tracie."

"You're right. Okay, Kee it is."

"Tell me about your daughter?" Kee asked.

"Well, she's adopted and she's six with chocolate skin and a big smile," Tracie said, smiling. "She is the light of my life."

"Do you live alone?" Kee asked

"Right now, I'm living with my sister."

"It must be hard raising a child in this age," Kee said.

The waitress brought their drinks and they both sipped at them lightly.

"It's not that bad. Well, give something up about yourself," Tracie said grinning.

"Okay. Let me see. I live alone, no kids, love my job and I'm unattached."

Tracie wondered briefly if Kee was flirting with her with that remark. The thought thrilled and frightened her. She decided she'd better go to a neutral topic. "Have you always wanted to be a gym teacher?" Tracie asked.

"That or a fly an airplane," Kee said.

Tracie took another sip of her drink. "Flying an airplane would be cool."

"My parents didn't think so. And since I was athletic but not really good enough to focus on any specific sport, here I am."

"Me, I always knew this was what I wanted since the fifth grade when I fell in love with my gym teacher," Tracie said.

"You know, I think most girls get a crush on their gym teacher."

"I suppose you're right."

They sipped their drinks while making idle conversation about the weather, sports and the school they worked at. Tracy had gotten very relaxed, so relaxed she started to feel sleepy.

"I hate to cut this short, but I'm more tired than I thought," Tracie said getting up.

Kee hurried and drank the rest of her drink. "Don't worry about it. We'll do it again, I'm sure."

They said their good nights as a cool breeze met them as they exited the bar.

***

When Tracie got home, Sam was watching television while Gail was reading the paper. "Hey, don't I get a hello?" Tracie stretched out her arms waiting for Sam to jump into them.

Sam got up and ran full steam ahead into Tracie's waiting arms.

"Mommy, I didn't hear you. I'm watching cartoons."

"Okay, fifteen more minutes and its bedtime." She kissed her on the forehead.

"How's it going, sis?" Tracie asked.

"Good," Gail answered.

"I'm bushed. I'm going to bed." Tracie headed for her room. "Could you put Sam to bed?"

"No problem," Gail said.

# The Admirer

The next morning Jody said goodbye to Ms. Jones and headed to work. When she arrived, Shawn was standing on the other side of the revolving door.

"Hey, you look nice," he said, smiling.

Jody grinned like a schoolgirl. "You look nice too."

"I'm here to remind you about our date for tonight."

"What date?" Jody said, teasing him.

"Well, Ms. Jones, it's the date I asked you for yesterday and you said yes."

"Let me think for a minute; you know my memory isn't that good," she said, beginning to laugh.

Shawn started laughing too. "Well, let me refresh your memory." He kissed her cheek. "How's that supposed to help me remember a date?" She was stunned that he had kissed her, as she tried to hide it.

"What I'm hoping is that the kiss was so good it jogged your memory and made you want another one tonight." His face got very serious, as he focused his light brown eyes on her. Jody suddenly grew uncomfortable and decided it was best to end this game. "I'll see you tonight. Here's my address. I'll be ready about seven."

Shawn smiled again, took her arm and escorted her to the elevator. They rode in silence and when the elevator door opened, he said he would see her tonight. She nodded, relieved he was gone for the time being. Karen was there when she arrived.

"Hey, don't take your coat off. Remember my case with the two women? Well, it seems our client the mother that has been accused of molestation is back in the house. She was told she couldn't be around children while the investigation was ongoing on. I need to go see what the situation is. You can be my witness and take notes. I would hate it if someone called Children Protective Services and the child got removed.

"Sure, I would love to go. It beats typing briefs all day," Jody said.

"By the way, their names are Sandy and Margo. The boy's name is Troy,"

"Which is being accused?" Jody gathered her briefcase with notepads and pens.

"Sandy."

When they arrived at the bi-level brownstone there was a Land Rover in the driveway. The walkway was lined with tulips all the way up to the door. When they knocked, a medium-built dark-skinned, woman answered. She was wearing an apron over her jeans. She dabbed her mouth with the bottom of the apron before she spoke

"Hello, can I help you?"

"I'm Karen Moore and this is Jody Jones. I'm representing Sandy," Karen said, reaching in her bag for a business card.

"Sandy's not home." She seemed to regret telling them that, by the look on her face. "Well, that's why I'm here. Sandy's not supposed to stay here. She was ordered by the court to reside somewhere else until her case is resolved," Karen said.

"So??" Margo said in a smart way.

"Well, we have sources that have seen the three of you dining out on one occasion, and her leaving here early in the morning on three other occasions."

"Well, your sources are all wrong. She only came by this morning after Troy went to school to pick up a few things." Margo seemed indignant about their accusations. "I think it's time for you to go."

"I'm only looking after her best interest," Karen said. "May we come in?"

Margo hesitated but then nodded and let them inside. Karen and Jody sat on the couch in the living room. Margo seemed nervous and remained standing.

As Jody looked around, she heard a faint shuffling coming from a back room.

Jody turned to Margo. "Are you sure she's not here? I think I heard something in the back of your house."

Margo hurried to the door and pulled it open. "It must be the cat. I think you should leave. "Okay, we're leaving," Karen said as they rose and walked back out to the front walkway.

Margo slammed the door behind them.

"Well, she's a piece of work," Jody said, getting into the passenger side of the car.

Karen was obviously mad. "Yeah, I don't know what's going on with those two. I was told by Sandy that they had broken up. If that's the case, what's she doing over here so much? And what about the court case?"

"Well, if they're broke up, Margo sure didn't act like it. I mean she would have ratted Sandy out for being over there if they were really at odds," Jody said.

"Let's get back to the office. I need to get in touch with Sandy to find out what the hell she's doing," Karen said turning up the music so she wouldn't have to talk while driving back to the office.

When they got back to the office, Jody went to her desk to type briefs. Karen quickly wrote up her findings from the visit and gave them to Jody to type.

They didn't leave the office for the rest of the day. They ate lunch at their desks and chatted when they needed a break.

When Jody got home, Diane was sitting in a chair in the living room watching television. "How was your day?"

"It was okay. Karen, the attorney I'm helping, has a child custody case involving two women breaking up, but get this—one is a teacher whose being accused of sexually abusing a student. It's very interesting," Jody said as she sat down in a chair.

"What do you want for dinner? I didn't know what to fix," Diane said as she rose from the chair.

"No, that's fine I'm going out for dinner." Jody said.

"Who do you have a date with?"

"Shawn, one of the litigators at the firm."

Jody got up to head to her bedroom. "I won't be late."

Diane called down the hall, "Be careful. Have a good time."

***

Jody went to her room to get ready. She looked through outfits, wondering what her dating life was like before the accident. She was nervous and apprehensive about being alone with Shawn outside of work.

She'd just finished dressing when Shawn arrived.

Diane answered the door.

"Hello, I'm Shawn Michaels. I'm here to pick up Jody."

Diane opened the screen door to let him in. "I'm Jody's mother, Ms. Jones. Please come in and have a seat."

Jody walked toward him. "Hello, Shawn."

He handed her a dozen roses. "You look very nice," Shawn said, smiling.

"So do you," Jody said, returning the smile.

They said goodnight to Diane and went out the door with Shawn's hand lightly pressing the small of Jody's back.

"Surprise," he whispered. There was a horse-drawn carriage waiting on the street.

"I thought since it was such a beautiful night that we'd ride to the restaurant." "This is nice, very nice," Jody said as Shawn helped her into the carriage. Her heart was thumping with excitement, and she felt special. The carriage and roses were a nice gesture. "Do you like seafood? The restaurant I picked is on the waterfront and the boat leaves in about an hour. If you'd rather have something different, we can go somewhere else," Shawn said.

"I guess I like seafood," Jody said timidly, not sure if she did or not.

"Hey, don't worry about it. I'm sure they have other stuff on the menu. How's work going?"

"Pretty good. Karen has a case that pretty interesting." She didn't want to elaborate on her role.

They were silent for a moment. "You know, I used to see you around and I always wanted to talk to you. I was an admirer that you never knew about."

Jody shifted in her seat. "Really?" She wasn't sure how to respond.

"Yeah, but you always seemed so untouchable. I mean your demeanor was like *stay away*."

"Really?" Jody again was not sure how to respond.

Shawn turned her face toward him. "I should have asked you this upfront. Are you seeing someone?"

Jody was dumbfounded because she didn't know how she wanted to answer that. "Shawn with my memory I can't answer that question. I'm taking things one day at a time. I don't know what surprises tomorrow may bring."

"Well, let me ask you this. Do you remember having a husband stashed away in a closet or a boyfriend that will come after me with an ax?" Shawn said, trying to lighten the mood.

Jody laughed at his joke. "No to both of your questions."

They arrived at the ship and Jody's eyes grew as wide as a child's at Christmas. "Wow, are we going on that?"

"Yep," Shawn said, seemingly happy. "Let's get aboard and find our table."

The boat was really a ship the size of a football field. It had chandeliers on every deck that were so bright you could probably see them from shore on a foggy day.

The ballroom was immaculately decorated for dinner. Shawn and Jody were shown to their table, and Shawn ordered a bottle of champagne. By the time the champagne was brought the ship's horn blew, signaling it was leaving port. Jody wanted to go on deck to see the stars and the ship leaving port. The music from inside made the outside even more romantic. The smell of the sea air brought back the memory that she'd always been fond of it.

"You wanna dance?" Shawn said, moving close to her and taking her in his arms.

"I'm not sure I remember how," Jody said, taking a step back.

"Don't worry I'll show you. Just follow me," Shawn said as he took her in his arms and moved ever so slowly.

Jody was very uncomfortable with the closeness of his body. "Shawn, I think you should be a little farther back."

"Well, I guess you remember something. I was just trying to get as close to you as possible. I've wanted this moment since the first day I saw you in the hall. Is this far enough?"

A whole person could stand between them.

"Yes. Why didn't you say anything to me before?" Jody said as she two stepped.

She realized Shawn was right. She did remember something

"Like I said before, you seemed to be untouchable to me," Shawn said while dipping her. Jody laughed because she didn't expect that move. She didn't say anything about what he'd said. She knew she should respond but something in her wouldn't let her say anything else.

They moved back inside. Jody tried to keep the conversation light as they waited for their dinner to be brought to them.

They polished off their lobster dinners and shared orange sherbet for dessert. The ship was pulling backing into port and the stars seem to shine brighter. There was no horse-drawn carriage ride home, but a car was waiting. When they arrived back at Jody's house, Diane was waiting up. She opened the door just as they approached.

"Did you all have a good time?" she asked.

"It was wonderful," Jody said.

"Well, it's late. You have work tomorrow." Diane said

The look on his face showed he hoped for more than just goodnight.

Jody turned toward him. He was standing in the doorway, not wanting to move yet. "I had a great time. I hope we can do it again sometime."

Shawn took the hint. "You bet we will. I guess I'll see you tomorrow." He turned to leave, and she noticed he seemed a little upset.

Diane went back to her chair. "He seems like a nice man."

"He is," Jody said. "You know something, he's very romantic. I mean we went to a waterfront restaurant by horse drawn carriage and had dinner on a ship that went out to sea."

"That sounds nice. He must really like you. Have you thought anything about Tracie? Why don't you ask her for lunch?"

*Wow where did that come from?* Jody wondered. "Sure, I'll ask her the next time I speak with her. I'm beat and it is a workday tomorrow." She headed down the hall.

# A Call From Richard

Gail's lawyer called the night before to let her know Richard would be calling this afternoon. Richard had asked for a private conversation with her. She briefly thought about fixing herself up then snapped out of that thought. It was a telephone call, not a date. She flopped down on the couch and watched the clock. Gail wondered what Richard wanted now and she fixed a drink to take the edge off. She knew it was early, but she was nervous about having to talk with Richard again. He had a way of making her feel like a child or someone with very limited intelligence.

The phone rang at exactly one. "Gail, Gail." Richard shouted.

"Yes, Richard," she said after untangling the phone wire.

"I was calling to see if we could have lunch. I'll be in the area sometime next week," he said in a commanding voice.

"Why? You mean your future wife won't mind you having lunch with your soon to be ex-wife again?" Gail said angrily.

"Like I tried to tell you, Gail, we're having some problems. This might sound strange, but I was hoping we could be friends. You know me, and I thought that maybe you could give me some advice."

"Why should I help you or give you advice after all you've done to me?" Gail said with hurt in her voice.

"Gail, I'm sorry. She's been going behind my back and talking to the lawyers. I keep telling her you're a reasonable person, but she doesn't believe me. You know how you women are. Petty. Gail, this is crazy. Why would I want to hurt you?"

Gail thought about what Richard was saying. She wasn't falling for his crap anymore. "Richard, I'm not the same trophy you dragged around in front of your friends. I am not the subservient person you made me into. If you have problems, then see a therapist like everyone else." She slammed the phone down, poured herself another drink and wondered what Richard really wanted. Gail was so upset she called Tracie.

# Sludge Coffee

Tracie was entering the school, forgoing her regular stop for coffee because she wasn't ready to interact with Kee. Tracie felt her phone vibrating in her pocket but couldn't get it out before the call went to voicemail. When she looked at it, she saw it was Gail.

She hurried and dialed the house number, thinking something must be wrong with Sam. Gail didn't get a chance to say anything before Tracie screamed, "What's wrong with Sam?"

"Nothing is wrong with Sam. I called you because Richard called," Gail said sheepishly. Tracie walked over to a corner so she wouldn't be overheard. "Why the fuck are you talking to that asshole?"

"I thought it might be something about the divorce," Gail said.

"If he wants to talk to you let him do what he's been doing... call your lawyer." Tracie was stern with her. "Don't be stupid, Gail. He's only trying to manipulate the situation. What happened to that vengeful woman you wanted to be?"

"She's still here," Gail said, sounding sleepy. "Just forget it. You're right. Who's picking up Sam?"

"I don't know if I have a meeting after work today, so maybe you should," Tracie said walking back into the chaos of kids going to their homeroom.

"Okay, no problem. See you later," Gail said as she hung up.

Tracie was the first one into the gym office. She made coffee then sat down on the couch to read the paper. Kee came in just as she was turning to the sports section.

"Good morning," Kee said cheerfully.

"Good morning to you. I made coffee if you like sludge," Tracie said turning in her direction.

"Me, I love it. I was walking down the street passing Starbucks and I thought why go in when Ms. Davis has got sludge waiting for me," Kee said, smiling.

"I want you to know this isn't just any sludge, but sludge made with special ingredients that I could be killed for if I told," Tracie said, beginning to laugh.

Kee poured the coffee; it came out the pot thick and midnight in color. "Mmm," she said as she looked in Tracie's direction.

"Okay, okay it's a little thick. Can we get to work and forget about my delicious coffee?" Tracie said getting up from the couch.

"Okay, let's get to work. But first I'm pouring that disgusting mess down the drain and hoping it doesn't clog it," Kee said, laughing.

After three classes of competition volleyball, it was lunch time.

"What have you got planned for lunch, Ms. Davis?" Kee asked as they put the gym equipment away.

"Well, nothing actually," Tracie said.

"Would you care to share a twelve-inch Subway sandwich with me?" Kee asked as they entered the office.

"Sure, what kind of sandwich do you like?" Tracie asked, sitting down.

"I like seven grain bread with turkey, provolone and the works except onion. I usually have them put honey mustard on it. What kind is your pleasure, Ms. Davis? I mean after seeing your coffee I don't know what you might want to eat." She grinned.

Tracie was almost speechless. She liked her sandwich the exact same way down to the honey mustard. "That sounds good to me," she answered, not wanting Kee to know it was her favorite sandwich, too. Who's going to get it?" Tracie asked.

"I'll go this time," Kee said as she headed for the door.

Tracie pulled out her cell phonee then dialed Jody's number.

"Hello."

"Hello, Ms. Jones. It's Tracie. Is Jody at home?"

"No, Tracie, she's at work."

"How's she doing?"

"Fine, she's doing fine," Ms. Jones said.

"Is she still seeing Dr. Stable?" Tracie asked.

"As far as I know, she is. Tracie why don't you come by Sunday for brunch? Jody was going to ask you the next time she talked to you."

Tracie couldn't believe her ears. Ms. Jones was asking her for brunch. She stumbled over her words. "Ye, Yes, of course. I'll be there. You sure it's okay with Jody?"

"I wouldn't ask you if I thought it was going to be a problem, but Tracie no talk of y'all or Sam. I just think maybe Jody could use somebody else to talk to besides me and the people she works with."

Tracie wasn't happy with the conditions, but she wanted to see Jody. "Of course. See you'll Sunday. Should I bring anything?"

"No, we'll see you Sunday." Ms. Jones hung up the phone.

***

Kee came in as Tracie wrapped up the conversation.

"I hope I didn't interrupt your call. You could have given me some kind of hand signal and I wouldn't have come in," Kee said.

"You're funny, really funny," Tracie said with a straight face.

Kee unwrapped the sandwiches and gave Tracie her half. "I bought two bottles of tea, if that's good for you."

"That's good for me," Tracie said as she took a big bite. The dripping honey mustard got on her chin.

"Let me get that," Kee said as she leaned over and dapped at the honey mustard on Tracie's chin with a napkin.

"Thanks." Tracie wished she would have asked first. It made her feel strange to have another woman touch her besides Jody.

The rest of the day was pretty routine with volleyball competitions and yelling kids. It was Friday, and they were both exhausted by the end of the day. They said their goodnights and they each went in a different direction. Tracie couldn't wait to tell Gail she would be seeing Jody on Sunday.

***

When Tracie got home, Sam was sitting on the floor doing homework with Gail.

"Mommy, Mommy," Sam said running as usual, full steam ahead.

Tracie swooped her up in her arms. "How's my girl?"

When Sam was back on solid ground she said, "When's Mommy Jody coming home? It's been days."

"The doctor still doesn't think she's ready to see anyone but Grandma."

"Can I talk to Grandma? Maybe she'd let me talk to Mommy anyway?"

"Sam, that would be going against doctor's orders. I know you miss her, but we have to be patient. Okay?"

"Okay," Sam said sadly.

"I tell you what we can do. After dinner, let's write her a letter."

Sam started jumping up and down. "Yippee, yippee, we're going to write to Mommy Jody."

When dinner was done, Sam got her paper and pencil and sat down next to Tracie on the couch.

"I'm ready," she said.

"Well, I see you are," Tracie said to her. "Okay, what do you want to say?"

"I want to say I love you and I want you to come home now. With a picture of my heart," Sam said.

Tracie eyes started to fill with tears, but she fought them back. "That sounds great, and I'm sure she misses you too."

Sam wrote her letter while Tracie watched her, thinking what a special girl she was.

Tracie's own heart was breaking each day despite trying to be patient with the whole situation. Tracie looked at Sam's picture of a huge heart with three figures inside it. She assumed the figures were her, Tracie and Jody holding hands. The picture reminded her of the many times they went to the zoo or park holding hands as they walked. The tears once again filled her eyes. She picked up a magazine to hide behind. Tracie felt like her life would never be complete again until Jody was back with her, but in that same moment of thought, Kee came to mind. She felt guilty that Kee came into her mind when she was thinking of Jody. She chalked it up to loneliness. She loved Jody and no one could take her place. She couldn't deny that there was something electrical between her and Kee. She realized that she hadn't told Kee about Jody because she was leaving the door open in case Jody didn't come back. She would never pursue Kee, but each day Jody seemed farther and farther away. She wanted Sunday to hurry and come. She put Sam to sleep with a bedtime story while Gail cleaned up the dishes. Finally, she was able to tell Gail her news.

"Guess what?" Tracie said to Gail smiling from ear to ear.

Gail saw the look on Tracie's face. "What has got you smiling like that?"

"I called Jody at Ms. Jones this afternoon and Ms. Jones invited me for brunch with her and Jody on Sunday."

"That's great." Gail said

"I just hope it turns out ok.

"It will. I'm turning in." Gail said

"Me too."

It seemed everyone had their own thoughts that night and wanted to be alone Tracie went to bed with visions of the life she used to have.

# NOVEMBER 2016

# The Branch

When Jody came home on Friday, Diane told her that Tracie called, and she invited her to brunch on Sunday.

"Diane, I wish you had asked me first. How do you know I didn't have a date?"

Diane sat down. "I'm sorry, I didn't think. I just thought it would be nice for you to talk to someone else besides your co-workers and me. Please forgive me. Do you want me to tell her not to come?"

Jody thought for a minute. "No, You already invited her maybe something she says will bring a memory."

"You never know. Let's get ready to eat."

***

Tracie was so nervous she clenched and unclenched her one free hand as she walked to Ms. Jones's door. She had a bouquet of roses in her other hand. She took one last look at herself before ringing the doorbell.

Ms. Jones opened the door. "Tracie, come in."

"Thank you."

Jody came from down the hall. "Hey Tracie."

"Thank you for having me." She handed Ms. Jones the bouquet of roses.

"Let's have a seat in the living room. Brunch is almost ready. Tracie, I hope you like quiche?" Ms. Jones asked.

"I love quiche; I don't care what kind it is. It sure smells good."

"I'll let you'll talk while I put the food on the table." Ms. Jones left the room.

"How's everything?" Tracie nervously asked.

"It's good. I'm working with Karen, a lawyer that has a custody case involving two women. One is a teacher that's accused of sexually abusing a girl student."

"Wow. That's deep. You always were an advocate for children. Are you practicing law?"

"No, Not yet. Right now, I'm reading law books and doing clerical stuff. Karen saw how interested I was in this case, so she keeps me in the loop."

"That sounds good but take it slow. That's the kind of case you loved; anything that involves children you were all over it."

"Really?

"Yeah, you didn't play when it came to protecting children."

"Wow, I felt like that when I read the brief for this case. Thanks for telling me that."

Ms. Jones came in and announced the food was on the table. There was a lot of small talk during brunch.

"What are y'all doing for Thanksgiving? Tracie asked.

Ms. Jones answered before Jody could open her mouth. "It's just going to be us."

"Thanksgiving?" Jody said

"Yeah, family gathering where you eat until you pass out. Y'all are more than welcome to join us. It's just going to be me, Sam and Gail my sister."

"Thank you, Tracie, but this year I want it to be just me and Jody. We have so much to be thankful for this year."

Tracie wanted to say something else but thought better of it. This is the first time Ms. Jones had been cordial to her. She didn't want to spoil the afternoon. "Well, it's an open invite if you change your minds."

"Thanks." They both said.

The brunch went well.

Tracie couldn't wait to get back to Gail's to tell her about brunch. It was just the two of them; Sam was visiting a friend for the afternoon.

"Gail, you are not going to believe this. Ms. Jones was nice. Overly nice. I couldn't believe it. She made a spinach quiche that was awesome. I kept pinching myself to make sure I wasn't dreaming."

"Hmm, I wonder what that was about?"

"I don't know but I will take it."

They both laughed and enjoyed the rest of the day watching movies.

# Sandy's Visit

# To Her Lawyer

Jody and Shawn had been having lunch and occasional dinners on a regular basis. She was quickly grasping what she needed in order to get back in front of a judge.

One day, walking into Karen's office, there was a person she didn't recognize sitting next to Karen. She only saw the back of the person's head but could tell the person was very agitated by the tone of her voice. When she got next to the person Jody did a double take; the female voice didn't match the rugged features she saw.

Jody cleared her throat hoping to give Karen a break from whatever the woman was saying.

"Jody, this is Sandy Morgan," Karen said turning toward her. "Have a seat and join us."

If it weren't for Sandy's voice, Jody wouldn't have been able to tell if the person was a man or woman. Sandy's build was stocky and masculine. She was dressed nicely, with a man's haircut.

Jody finally spoke. "It's nice to meet you."

"Same here," Sandy said

Karen turned back to Sandy. "As one of your lawyers, I'm telling you that the court ordered you to stay away from your house. If you don't want to go to jail, then you better start doing it. All it takes is one person to report you."

"I just went by there that one time. I swear," Sandy said, squirming in her chair.

"Please don't give me that garbage. We have witnesses who saw you at a restaurant with Margo and Troy," Karen said raising her voice a little.

"What can I say? I missed Troy."

"I understand that, but if you want to stay out of jail you have to stay away. What about the custody case? The way Margo talked when we were over there, the two of you are a couple again."

She turned toward Karen with a hardened face. "Margo and I are through. She's just putting on a front for you. I don't know what kind of game she's playing, but all I want is Troy. I guess she wants everyone to see how nice she is. I can't tell you what her motives are. This whole thing is such bullshit. I would never hurt a child. I love children. That's what got me into teaching in the first place. Why would I jeopardize everything? That kid needed attention and I showed her some, and this is how I get repaid."

Jody couldn't help but speak. "I understand how you feel, but allegations have to be investigated. You may not be a child molester but how will anyone know you're innocent of the charges unless there is a thorough investigation?"

"I know, I know but I just can't believe that she took my kindness and turned it against me," Sandy said in anger.

"Maybe you were a little too kind," Karen said to her. She wanted to see if anything came out that shouldn't.

"The kid would fall asleep in class, and her clothes looked like they hadn't been washed in months. I called her parents in four times. They had the same excuse that she was sneaking and watching television late at night. They'd wake her up for school and as soon as they left for work, she must have went back to bed. The mother says she wears wrinkled clothes because it is her daughter's chore to wash her own clothes and she refuses. Everytime her parents came to my classroom they reeked of alcohol. So, I'm guilty of caring by helping her with her homework and giving her a sandwich," Sandy said throwing up her hands.

"She's a street smart twelve-year-old. A little girl that thinks she's an adult. One of the other lawyers on the team interviewed her and she says that more went on than homework and sandwiches. She said you tried to touch her breast and go under her skirt," Karen said sitting back waiting for her response.

Sandy was angry. Her face grew red. "What the fuck is she talking about?

Nothing happened. If I broke any rule, it was giving her a sandwich after school."

Jody turned toward her. "Sandy, let Karen do her job and everyone will know you're innocent. It's the only way."

Sandy stood. "I'm outta here. Call me when you have something."

Karen stood also. "Just stay away from your house. Karen sat back down near Jody.

"What's your take on her?" she asked Jody.

"You know, Karen, I couldn't tell if she was a man or woman when I first walked in."

Karen laughed. "She's a woman. You had a gay friend before your accident, and from what I gather, someone named Tracie. She was your best friend. You know people talk"

"Really," Jody said, wondering exactly what people said about her.

"Yes, really," Karen said.

"I don't remember any of it," Jody said getting up and heading to her office. Karen followed to pick up some typed briefs. When the clock on the wall struck twelve, there was a knock at the door.

***

Shawn came in pushing a table for lunch. "Hey beautiful. What's up beside me bringing you lunch?"

Karen laughed and grabbed her purse. "I'm out. Three's a crowd."

"It's just you and me," Shawn said, pushing the table over by the window so they could look at the hustle and bustle below.

Jody sat down across from him and thought about how considerate and attentive he'd been in the short while she'd spent time with him. "Shawn, how's work?" She still wanted to keep the conversation on neutral ground.

Shawn picked up his burger. "Good, one of my boys on Karen's team told me about the case you're working on."

Jody picked up her burger and in between chews said, "It's very interesting. I mean two women being together with a child. The accused woman was here earlier."

"Yeah, what did you think of her?" he asked putting down his burger and holding her with his eyes.

Jody kept eating. "She was okay. I mean, she was angry about the allegations and not being able to spend time with her son."

"Yeah, that's a shame but what's your take on the family thing?"

"I don't feel one way or another. I don't understand it," Jody said putting down her burger and looking at it on the plate. She didn't know why she felt a sudden stab of guilt.

"You know Jody, I feel the same way. I mean those people can do whatever they want as long as they don't try to push up on me with it," Shawn said

Jody grew uncomfortable. "Shawn, can we change the subject if you don't mind?"

"No, I don't mind." He seemed happy with her response. "How about dinner and a movie this weekend?"

"Sure, that sounds good," Jody said smiling.

They finished their lunch with idle chit chat and before long the clock struck one and it was time to get back to work. Shawn rolled the table to the door. When Jody tried to open it Shawn held it closed. He leaned across the table and kissed her on the lips. She held her breath, unable to move, and returned his kiss.

"Thank you," Shawn said in a sexy whispering voice.

"For what?" Jody said, still pinned against the wall.

"For not backing away," Shawn said.

"I'll see you later," Jody said, trying to get him out of the office before Karen came in. She didn't want anyone getting the wrong idea about Shawn because something in her said this was wrong.

Karen entered. "Ready to get back to work?" she said, going to sit on the couch to look at her papers. "How's it going with Shawn?"

"He's so nice. What do you know about him?" Jody sat down.

"Well, he's every girl's dream man around here. He's not married and doesn't have baby mama drama."

"What do you mean, baby mama drama?" Jody asked.

"It means he doesn't have babies out there whose mothers are trying to milk him for every cent he has," Karen said.

"We've had lunch and dinner together a couple of times, but that's all."

"I can tell by the way he looks at you that he's hooked. And from what I hear he's always had a thing for you."

"You know, he said something similar over dinner one night. He said I seemed untouchable," Jody said.

"From what I heard, Jody, you didn't give any of the guys here any time. They figured you were seeing someone on the outside," Karen said. "Like maybe, Tracie?"

"What, are you serious?" She flushed profusely.

Karen handed her some briefs and stood. "Take my advice, don't let him get away. He's nice, considerate, attentive and likes you a lot."

Jody didn't say anything. She took the briefs and went to her desk to type them. She called Dr. Stable for an appointment the next day. She had been skipping appointments. She was glad the doctor hadn't called Diane to find out why.

***

Jody could see Diane peeking out the window as she walked up the walkway. Diane opened the door, and all Jody could see was red roses. They were on the floor, in vases, and on every table available in the living room.

"What's all of this"? Jody asked.

"They're for you."

"For me? From whom?"

"Shawn Michaels." Diane said.

"Was there any message?" Jody asked.

"Thanks for lunch," Diane said. "What was so special about lunch?"

"Nothing that I know of," Jody said hanging up her coat and heading to the kitchen. They both sat down. Diane was heating dinner in the oven. The smell of the chicken was familiar. Jody couldn't wait to eat.

Diane turned toward her as she was stirring the pot. "Have you been to your sessions lately?"

Jody felt like a child who had skipped school. "No, I've been so busy at work I've missed a session or two."

Diane stopped stirring. "Jody, you know how important those sessions are."

"Yeah, I know. I have an appointment tomorrow morning."

"Well, I'm glad to hear that," Diane said placing a piping hot plate of braised chicken and gravy with mashed potatoes in front of Jody.

"No veggies?" She smiled while looking down at her plate.

"You know better than that." Diane took the salad from the refrigerator and sat down to join her. "I thought I'd tell you a little more about your father while we eat. He was a handsome man with skin color of chocolate and the whitest teeth you ever seen. He was 6 ft tall, and loved to dress. That man could make a suit talk when he put it on. Jody, loved you so, so much. You were everything to him. The military helped him make a good living for us. We never wanted for anything, not a thing. I wish you could remember him. He was so proud of being your father. He told anyone that would listen about any accomplishment you made and sometimes twice if the person didn't find a way from him. Then he got lung cancer and it took him from us." Diane dabbed at her eyes to keep the tears from falling.

"I wish I could remember him," Jody said sadly patting Diane's hand then getting up from the table. She thanked Diane for dinner and headed to her room for some relaxation.

# A Visit To

# Dr. Stable's Office

Jody arrived at Dr. Stable's office bright and early. The receptionist called her name before she could sit. She entered Dr. Stable's office, noticing her massive desk. There was a picture of her husband with a loving message to his wife, and a picture of her two kids. Her walls were covered with framed degrees.

A clutter of papers surrounded them.

Dr. Stable asked her to have a seat.

Jody sat nervously, crossing her legs.

"How's it been going? I haven't seen you in a while."

"It's been going good. I'm working and getting out," Jody said.

"That's good. But you know Jody, these sessions are very important."

"Yes, I'm know, but I've been so busy with work that I'm worn out by the time I get off," Jody said, trying to reason with her.

"I understand, but these sessions are important to your well-being."

"I just don't think I need to come so much anymore." Jody blurted out.

"I suppose you like your life, and you don't care about your life before the accident. You know your life before the accident could have been just as good or even better."

Jody was getting flustered. "I, I do like my life. I'm seeing this guy, Shawn, from work, who is very nice, and things are good."

"Do you really think it's a good idea to get involved when you have so much unresolved?"

"I don't know. Everything is happening so fast," Jody said, unsure of herself now.

"Are you remembering things?"

Jody felt like she was getting a headache with all the questions. "Some."

"What kind of things?"

"Yesterday, I remembered the smell of Diane's chicken cooking. And I remembered I liked the smell of the sea." She said fidgeting with her purse. "I've been remembering things, but the thoughts don't seem to be connected to one another.

"The connection will come you have to give it time. Maybe you should start on that journal we spoke about before. You might think that it won't help but you need to give it a chance. I want you to write down anything you remember and see if you can connect to something else you wrote. Jody, you need to look at your writings every day. You don't know what's going to put it all together.

"I guess I could do that," Jody said, knowing she really wasn't

"What's important is that you recognize which thoughts go together." Dr. Stable clasped her hands together. "Tell me about your job."

Jody relaxed. "I'm learning and helping. They aren't letting me argue any cases or anything like that but Karen, one of lawyers, has a case of two women in a custody fight and one's been accused of child molestation.

"Really, that is interesting," Dr. Stable said. "Is this case bringing back any thoughts for you?"

"No, not really. I mean I feel sorry for the accused woman," Jody said.

"What do you mean when you say you feel sorry for her?"

"I mean she seems nice and not like someone who would do something like that." Jody felt herself growing impatient.

"Does a person that has molested a child have a certain look?" Dr. Stable asked.

Jody was suddenly sorry she hadn't left the conversation about her job at *fine*.

"Dr. Stable, could we drop the subject? I'm not here to analyze the case. I've got my own issues to deal with."

They talked for a while longer before Dr. Stable stood, signaling the end of the session. "Jody you seem to be adjusting to your new life well, but you still need to know your old life before you throw it away. Come back in a month with your journal."

Jody stood, glad that it was over.

Dr. Stable opened the door. "See you next time."

"Bye." Jody walked out and was glad for the freedom of the outdoors. She thought about her session as she walked to the bus stop. She knew Dr. Stable was right; she needed to know what her previous life was about before she could move on with her new life. Hell, she might have even liked her old life. She stopped at a bargain store that had shoes all thrown in a bin. She wondered if Dr. Stable's life was a mess like all the shoes thrown in the bin. Wouldn't that be something?

Jody kept walking, enjoying the sunshine, and thinking about her new life. She wondered if Shawn was going to be part of her future, and when she would have her own cases. The bus finally came, and she got on with thoughts of her future.

# Sisterly Love

Gail heard from her lawyer, and she was hopping mad when she got off the phone. Richard now wanted to sell the house. He wass asking the court to petition her to give a breakdown of her financial situation to see if she could afford the house.

Gail poured herself a drink and sat down and cried. What a fool she had been for all those years, she thought. And now she's about to get kicked out of her house. She picked up the phone to dial Tracie but put it back down. How was she going to tell her sister that she didn't have a red cent? Gail picked up the phone again, and with no choice, dialed Tracie.

Tracie was sitting down talking with Kee when she saw Gail's number on her cell. She excused herself and went into the hallway. She couldn't imagine what Gail could want. She just hoped it wasn't anything bad.

"Hey, sis. What's up?"

"That bastard is trying to take this house," Gail said in tears.

"What?" Tracie asked not understanding what Gail meant.

Gail started crying even harder. "I, I don't have any money to keep this house.""What about the pre-nup?" Tracie asked.

"It's in the pre-nup that we would split the proceeds from the house if I can't afford it. Tracie, I told you about this."

"Yeah, I remember. I'm sorry Gail I just have so much on my plate with this thing with Jody."

"What am I going to do?"

"Do you have anything?" Tracie asked not believing that her sister hadn't put something away for a rainy day.

Gail said in a whisper not having the strength to say the words any louder. "No, nothing. I never thought Richard would leave me. I was stupid not to confront him about all his affairs. I thought as long as it was outside it didn't matter; he'd come to his senses one day. Tracie, I feel like such a fool. I just took whatever he gave me and was satisfied." The tears fell fast down Gail's face.

Tracie couldn't stand the thought of Richard hurting her sister. She knew she needed to go home to comfort her. She'd been there for her when she needed a shoulder. "I'm coming home right NOW!"

"No, don't. I had a drink and I'm going to have another and hopefully go to sleep." "Okay, but call me when you get up," Tracie said.

Gail sounded defeated "Yeah."

Tracie went back into the office. Today was another administrative day. There was paperwork to be done.

Kee saw how sad Tracie looked when she came in. "Is everything alright?"

"It'll be okay as soon as my sister is divorced from that bastard husband of hers," Tracie blurted then realizing she was exposing herself.

"You should be with her," Kee said with concern.

"You know, you're right," Tracie said as she gathered up her things then left.

***

Tracie felt a strong urge to speak to Jody. Jody had the level head in times like these. She dialed the number even though she knew she was probably at work.

"Hello" Jody said a little breathless as if she'd just ran.

"Hi, it's Tracie." She was a little tongue tied because she had expected Ms. Jones. "How are you?"

"I'm good, thanks for asking," Jody said politely.

"You must be really busy because you're always out when I call." Tracie said pulling over to the shoulder of the road.

"Yeah, work has been really busy."

"I see. Have you been going to see Dr. Stable?"

"Actually, I just came from seeing her."

"How'd it go? Are you remembering anything?" She was anxious to find out.

"A few things here and there," Jody said.

"That's great! How does it feel?" Tracie asked smiling.

"It feels... a bit odd. But overall good."

"Have you remembered anything about me or Sam?

"No, nothing like that." She sounded guarded again and Tracie's heart sank.

"How's things with Diane?" Tracie asked.

"Fine things are good with Diane. You are full of questions," Jody said smartly.

"I can't help it. I... miss you." Tracie cleared her throat. "I was wondering if we could grab a bite to eat this weekend."

Jody stammered. "I, I got a date this weekend."

Tracie got mad as hell when she heard that. She took a deep breath and remembered what Gail said. "Well, how about the following weekend?"

"I guess that will be okay," Jody said hesitantly.

Tracie turned back on to the road. "I'll pick you up about seven, Saturday after this weekend." Tracie said smiling.

"Let's make it lunch," Jody said.

"Whatever you want. I'm just glad I get to see you." Tracie said.

"Okay, I gotta go. I'll see you."

Tracie was in heaven. Finally, she would get to see Jody alone. When she got home, Gail was

sprawled out on the couch with an empty shot glass on the coffee table.

Tracie tried to tiptoe into the kitchen, but she bumped into an end table.

Gail sat up, rubbing her eyes. "What are you doing here?"

Tracie didn't want her to feel ashamed. "I had an administrative day, so I got out early."

"Oh." Gail reached for the tequila.

Tracie took the bottle from her. "The answer's not in the bottle. It looks like you already had a few and the problem is still here."

"True, but for a little while I forgot all about my problems," Gail said.

"Gail, we'll deal with this together. Richard is not going to get the house." Tracie said, acting like the big sister. I have some money saved and you can ask that the divorce hearing be moved up so the matter of the pre-nup and divorce can get settled faster."

"Trace, I can't take your money. I know you and Jody are saving for a house." She put her head in her hand and looked up at Tracy. "I decided, I'm going to agree to sell," Gail said choking back tears.

This was breaking Tracie's heart. "How much is the house payment?"

"It's three thousand a month for the house and utilities."

"Gail, you know Jody, she would have been to the bank by now giving you all our money. The way things look we won't be buying a house anytime soon."

With tears falling from her eyes. "Trace, I don't know what to say."

"Just take the money. You'll be good for about a year. Tell your lawyer to let Richard know that your sister is moving in with you to help with the bills. And the bills are not a problem."

Gail gave Tracie a big hug. "I want to thank you," she said with tearing running down her cheeks.

"Please stop crying. This is only a temporary fix. Your lawyer has to get that date moved up. I can't believe there are that many divorces going on," Tracie said looking at the clock.

"I think Richard is having his lawyer stall in hopes that I forget the pre-nup and take whatever money he offers."

"Well, your lawyer better start earning his pay. By the way, how did you get such a big-time lawyer with no money?" Tracie asked curiously.

"I pawned some of my jewelry. Richard is an asshole, but he bought me expensive jewelry, so I'd look nice when he took me out."

"Well, you might have to pawn some more of it if this goes beyond a year."

"I don't wanna think about it right now," Gail said.

"I don't want to get into your business, but what are you planning to do with yourself? No matter how this comes out you will need something to fill your days. Sam and I have to go home sometime. I think you should get a job."

Gail stepped back. "I know, Trace, but I don't know how to do anything."

"You're good with kids. You're a good organizer, and you're good at decorating. You just have to put yourself out there."

"You're right. But if I win, I won't need to." Gail said.

Tracie couldn't believe her. Gail was a sweetheart, but she was spoiled.

Gail wouldn't admit it, but she liked being spoiled by Richard. Why else would she have put up with him?

"Who's picking up Sam?" Gail asked changing the subject.

"We still got time. Did you hear what I just said?" Tracie said sternly.

"Yes, I heard you."

"Why don't we both pick Sam up? She'll love that." Tracie said lightening the mood.

# Tracie and Kee

When Tracie entered the office the next day, Kee was already there. "Hey, co-gym teacher, is everything okay?"

"Yeah, for right now it is. Thanks for taking care of things here," Tracie said.

"No problem." She handed Tracie a cup of steaming coffee.

Tracie blew on it and sipped. "Mmmm, this is good."

"How would you know, after that sludge you try to pass of as coffee," Kee said laughing.

"Hey, it might be sludge, but its good sludge," Tracie said. "And since you have a problem with it, from now on coffee is your job."

Kee sat her coffee down and looked at Tracie. "Are you dictating? Is that how you treat all your

relationships?"

Tracie was taken aback by the word *relationship*. "We don't have a relationship." "Yes, we do. A working relationship," Kee said smiling. "You don't have to look so scared.

"I wasn't scared. I knew what you were talking about," Tracie said defensively

"I bet." Kee picked up her coffee. She spent the rest of the day teasing Tracie about their conversation.

Tracie again felt that Kee was coming on to her. She felt that Kee had enjoyed seeing her squirm a little while ago. Tracie was wondering what her game was. She'd kept things light and business-like at school because she didn't want to send any mixed signals no matter how curious she was. She had to admit to herself that Kee would have her interest if she weren't married.

# Jody's and Diane Conversation

Jody was sitting by the window peeking out when Diane arrived home from a doctor's appointment.

Jody had the door open before she could put the key in.

"This is a surprise, you waiting for me."

"How was your doctor's appointment?" Jody asked. She was concerned.

"It was alright, but what's on your mind to have you so concerned with my health? Am I kicking the bucket and the doctor forgot to tell me?" She grinned.

"No, of course not. I wanted to run something by you. I agreed to see Tracie for lunch the Saturday after this." Jody hung Diane's coat.

Diane walked over to her favorite chair and sat down. "Why?"

Jody sat on the couch facing her. "I saw Dr. Stable and she said that if I want to live this new life, I need to at least know what my old life was like."

"Jody, I want you back with me forever and I'll do anything for that to happen. I want to fill all those blank spaces in your brain. I want there to be no questions about your life."

Jody was expecting her to say something much different. What that was she didn't know. "I'm going to take a nap. All this stuff is just too much. I feel like my brain is going to explode."

"You're not eating?" Diane asked.

"No," Jody said heading to her bedroom.

# Question

The first four days of the week went pretty uneventful for Jody, and then came Friday.

She was typing some briefs when Sandy came in.

"Is Karen here?" she asked politely.

Jody turned from her computer. "No, I'm sorry, Sandy, but she's out on another case."

Sandy sat down with her head in her hands. "I need this nightmare to end."

Jody didn't know what to say to console her except, "Hang in there."

"That's easy for you to say because you're not living this mess. I can't see my son and that bitch Margo is accusing me of ruining her reputation."

"I know things seem to be moving slowly but they're interviewing people as fast they can.

There are a lot of people not making themselves available," Jody said.

"Like who?" Sandy asked bolting straight up in her chair.

"Look, I've said too much already so please come back when Karen is here."

Sandy stood up. "Thanks anyway, for your help."

When it was near time for Jody to leave, she stopped by Karen's office to leave a note that Sandy had stopped by.

***

Shawn was right on time to pick her up that evening. This time, to impress her, he had rented a limousine to take her to dinner at a swanky restaurant in mid-town.

As Jody stepped into the limousine, she caught sight of a bottle chilling in a bucket and heard soft music playing. "You sure go all out on a date," she said to him.

Shawn stepped in after her. "For only you," he said, sitting close to her. Then he had a thought. "Are you game for something silly?"

"Silly how?"

"Well, I just thought maybe we'd just drive around Manhattan and have hot dogs and champagne," He said showing his pearly whites.

"Are you serious?" she grinned back at him

"As a heart attack, but only if you want to. I mean we do have reservations at one of the hottest restaurants in Manhattan." He loosened his tie.

"Well, since you're already getting undressed. I guess its champagne and hot dogs." "Jody, if I were getting undressed, we wouldn't be riding around in no limousine. We'd be in my apartment."

Jody moved over an inch or so. "Whoa there. I was only kidding."

Shawn looked at her with dreamy eyes. "I wasn't."

Jody quickly changed the subject. "So where do we get hot dogs this time of night?"

"Well, I know this place that stays open twenty-four hours a day and it serves the best hot dogs in town," he said with a grin.

Jody was getting nervous. "Where? I don't like surprises."

Shawn took her hand. "I would never do anything to hurt you. I have waited since the first day I saw you to get this opportunity. If where we're going is not okay, then we'll leave."

Jody cleared her throat. "Well, then I guess it's okay."

They drove around giggling like school kids until finally the limo stopped.

Jody looked out the window and saw a high-rise building.

She was a little tipsy. "Where are we?"

Shawn reached over and kissed her gently on the lips. "My house."

Things were happening too fast. "Shawn, I'm not ready."

Shawn looked into her eyes and closed her hand in his, "No pressure, just hot dogs and champagne. Don't be afraid. The driver will be waiting to take you home whether it's ten minutes from now or ten hours."

Jody was scared, but she didn't know why. Shawn had been nothing but attentive and romantic. She even fantasized about where their relationship might go. She couldn't finish the thought; it was too unimaginable to her.

"Okay," she said. The ride up to his apartment was quiet with him holding her hand. The apartment was decorated with a masculine taste—black leather couches, chairs, and glass tables in the living room.

"Have a seat," Shawn said as he got a remote off the table and dimmed the lights in the living room. Then he started the fireplace and soft jazz came through the speakers on the walls. "Excuse me a few minutes while I put some hot dogs on," he said walking down a short hallway.

"Sure," Jody said as she sank into the sofa.

Shawn came back in with a bottle of champagne. "The hot dogs will be ready in fifteen minutes. What would you like on yours?"

"Mustard and relish if you have it, but no more champagne for me; I've had my limit." He put the champagne down. "Yep, I have both mustard and relish. Can I show you the rest of the apartment?"

"Sure," Jody said getting off the couch and following him.

The kitchen had new appliances and the bathroom had double sinks and a shower with tinted shower doors.

"This is nice," Jody said, heading back toward the living room because she didn't want to go any further.

Shawn followed her but stopped at the kitchen. He shouted from the kitchen, "Yeah, it is, but its missing something."

"What else could you possibly need?" Jody asked.

"Well, actually two things: someone to share it with and someone to redecorate." Shawn walked out of the kitchen with two plates with hot dogs.

"Redecorate? But it seems like your personality," Jody told him.

"I doubt that any woman would go for it."

"You're probably right," Jody said taking a bite of a hot dog. "This is delicious. How'd you do it?"

"The secret is beer. Add a little to the boiling water. Now that you know my secret you have to share your life with me."

"Not so fast, but we'll see," Jody said finishing one hot dog to start on the other.

"That's good enough for right now." Shawn said, looking at her with dreamy eyes again.

Jody felt, once again, that she'd better change the subject. "Where did you get the furniture from?"

"Ethan Allen."

"Who? I don't know him," Jody said.

Shawn fell over laughing. "It's not a person. It's a furniture store."

Jody felt a little stupid. "I guess we should leave. It's getting late."

Shawn stopped laughing and put on a straight face. "I'm sorry I laughed."

Jody put down her hot dog. "No, it's not that. It's just getting late."

Shawn took both of Jody's hands in his and whispered, "You know you could stay the night.

There is a spare room."

"Shawn, no. I told you before I'm not ready and I would like to leave," Jody said impatiently.

Shawn let her hands go and rose from the couch. "Okay, I am a man of honor. If I tell you something that's the way it is. Let me call the driver and have him bring the car around."

They rode the elevator in silence, a silence that continued on the drive to Jody's. Shawn gave her a peck on the cheek as she got out of the car. He waited until she was safely behind closed doors then left.

Jody closed the door and saw there was a night light on in each room, so she'd be able to see in the darkness. How sweet Diane was to do something like that. She would have to thank her tomorrow, but for now she couldn't wait to crawl under her covers.

# An Unexpected Conversation

The next workday, when Jody arrived at her building for work, it was Sandy, not Shawn who greeted her.

"Hey, can I speak to you for a minute?" Sandy asked.

Jody didn't want to be seen with her because she looked so masculine. "There's a coffee shop around the corner. I'll meet you there, but I don't think I'm the person you should be talking to."

Sandy's face grew soft. "I know, but something about you tells me you're the person I need to

speak to. I promise it won't take long."

"Okay," Jody said turning around to go back through the revolving door. She wondered why she agreed to meet with her. She couldn't help her.

Sandy had walked ahead of her and was already sitting in a booth when Jody came in.

"I took the liberty of ordering you coffee," Sandy said.

Jody just wanted to get to the point. "I'm already late. What can I help you with?"

"I was hoping that you'd speak to Karen about me seeing my son," Sandy said looking into her coffee.

"Why me?" Jody asked curiously.

"Because I think she might a have problem with me being gay." She looked Jody straight in the eyes.

"I can tell you that Karen treats you just like any other client. And how do you know I don't have a problem with you being gay?"

"My gay-dar," Sandy said.

"Your what?"

"It's something that gay people have. The ability to recognize another gay person," Sandy said.

Jody pushed the cup of coffee away. "Well, your gaydar is off. I have a boyfriend and like I said you should be talking to Karen."

Sandy got up from the booth. "I hope there are no hard feelings. I obviously made a mistake.

It happens. Thanks for your time."

Jody left the restaurant in a huff.

When she got back to the office, she told Karen part of what had happened. She only said that Sandy wanted to see her son. Karen said she would do what she could to get supervised visits for her, but until then Sandy needed to stay away. The case was progressing and most of the people that needed to be interviewed finally had been completed. Jody was glad. She didn't want to see Sandy anytime soon. She had accused her of liking women, and it bothered her. She finished out her day keeping to herself, and she declined Shawn's offer for lunch. She pulled out the picture of her, Sam, and Tracie. Why? She asked herself.

# Tracie and Jody Have A Date

For Tracie, time seemed to move as fast as a turtle. But eventually, the day of her date with Jody had come. She asked Gail to take Sam out because she couldn't concentrate on anything but the upcoming lunch. It had to go right.

Tracie wanted to pick Jody up, but Jody said she'd meet her since she was going to be downtown away. Tracie didn't ask, but she assumed Jody had a session with Dr. Stable. Smack Your Lips Ribs was close by, and it was one of Jody's favorite restaurants.

When Jody walked in wearing skinny jeans and a fitted coat, Tracie's heart skipped a beat. Jody sat down across from her in the booth.

"Thanks for coming," Tracie said.

"No, thank you for inviting me. Was this my favorite restaurant?" She asked.

Tracie grinned, pleased that she seemed so relaxed. "Well, one of them. And just like the name says, you always smacked you lips when you were finished. Actually, you not only smacked your lips, but you licked your fingers too."

Jody burst out laughing. She couldn't imagine doing that. She felt the waves of her laughter deep in her chest. It felt good. She watched with wide eyes as the waitress placed overflowing plates of BBQ beef ribs, fries and slaw in front of them. She inhaled the aroma. "Wow, this smells delicious."

"Dig in and don't hold back," Tracie encouraged.

Tracie bought Jody's favorite wine with her because there was a BYOB policy at the restaurant. Tracie poured the red wine into their glasses and made a simple toast to memories forgotten. She loved to see Jody eat. It was like watching a starving construction worker. She just kept shoveling it in. "Hey, slow down before you choke."

Jody just grinned.

Tracie raised her glass to make another toast. "To remembering," she said.

"To the sun and moon," Jody said.

Tracie blinked in disbelief. That was something Jody always said when they drank. She remained cool even though her heart felt like it was going to beat right out of her chest. "Why'd you say that?"

Jody stopped eating and licked her fingers. "I don't know; it just came out."

Tracie knew their relationship was fragile, so she let it go, but she had to know whether

Jody was remembering things. "How's your sessions going?"

Jody took a sip of wine. "Good."

"Are you remembering anything before the accident?" Tracie asked.

"Things here and there, but the connection is what's missing. Dr. Stable has me keeping a journal," Jody said.

"That's a good idea. Have any of what you've remembered had to do with me or Sam?"

"Hey, let's just enjoy these ribs."

"I'm not trying to pressure you. I just thought if you were having any thoughts or confusion as to what the relationship between you, me and Sam was maybe you should meet her," Tracie said

taking a sip of her wine. "I mean, what better way to connect your thoughts than up close and personal."

Jody stopped eating and sat quietly. The picture in her desk came to mind. "Sure," she said.

"Why not? Maybe it's time I met her." She paused. "I'm glad we did this."

Tracie agreed. Then she pretended to be the interested friend by asking, "How's things going with you and Shawn?"

"It's great. We see each other every day, and we talk every night. You know, Tracie, he's just so understanding, so loving."

"Do you love him? I mean so much has happened in the last couple of months." Tracie's voice cracked. Jody gave her a don't go there look.

"I don't honestly know. I know I like him a lot. But every time he gets close, something pulls me back." She stared at the naked rib bones on her plate.

Tracie's heart soared an inch or two just knowing that maybe, just maybe, something was holding her back. "Hey, give yourself time. Don't push it." But inside she was thinking *come back to me. I'm dying without you.* "When is a good time for you to meet Sam?"

"How about the first Saturday after Thanksgiving?"

"Sure," Tracie said as she watched Jody stand. "Hey, the invite for you and Diane to come over Thursday still stands."

"I gotta run," Jody said.

"Do you have to go? I was hoping we could go to a movie or take a walk."

"I wish I could, but I have other plans. Bye, have a good Thanksgiving"

Tracie watched her walk out the door. She wanted to savor the time they had so she poured

another glass of wine and daydreamed about what used to be.

***

When she got home, it was late. She had driven around going nowhere in particular. She saw

Sam's light was off when she entered the house and knew she was sleep. The only light that was

on came from a small lamp in the living room that Gail used for reading. Gail looked up from

her book when she heard footsteps. "How'd it go?"

"Short," Tracie said going over to the bar to fix a drink. "You want one?'

"Sure, why not? It's been one of those days. Did she at least stay for lunch?" Gail asked.

"Yeah, it was good. Gail, seeing her made me miss her even more. I'm trying to be patient but damn, I don't know how much more I can take."

"Shh, you don't want to wake Sam. I know it's hard but you gotta hang in there.

"Anything happening with Richard's bullshit?"

"Well, my lawyer says we should be able to mediate the case in a couple of weeks rather than waiting for a judge to hear the case. The problem only comes if we still want to contest the pre-nup. I agreed to whatever will get this nightmare over with. I'm tired of playing games. Let's mediate. We're waiting on Richard to say yes," Gail said.

Tracie went and kissed her sister on the cheek. "Take your own advice and hang in there. I'm going to bed."

***

Tracie left for work early the next morning. Gail was taking Sam to the bus and would pick her up since she was lunching with her lawyer. When Tracie entered the office, there was a note on

the desk. The note said, I have an appointment today that I forgot about. I'll be out but let me make it up to you with drinks after work for the short notice. If you can make it, meet me at The Girls Club on Thirty-Fifth Street, Kee.

Tracie was intrigued by the note wondering through out the day what it really was about. When the day was finally over she headed to the bar. Tracie sat at the bar when she got to the club. The Girls Club was an upscale gay jazz club. It's only a drink, she reasoned. It seemed strange being out without Jody. She didn't want to give Kee the wrong impression, but at the same time Tracie felt flattered. She called Gail and told her she was going out with friends. She didn't want Gail to think her meeting with Kee was something it wasn't, though she found herself thinking more about Kee than she should. What Tracie realized was that she had to step up her game to get Jody back. No matter how many women interested her there was only one Jody, although she still wondered about Kee.

Tracie saw Kee come in. "Hey, thank you for the invite."

"I'm glad you came. What are you drinking?" Kee asked.

"Just a cranberry juice. I was waiting for you. What made you think I was gay? I mean, you must have suspected something to invite me here," Tracie asked.

"Where'd that come from? I mean slow down. Take a breath. I was taking a chance by asking you here. But you just confirmed it," Kee said.

Tracie sipped her drink. "Girl, I tell you, you're real smart."

"I know. Do you wanna eat or run?" Kee asked.

"Running sounds pretty good but my stomach needs food. Let's eat," Tracie said. "There's only one thing. If you stay for the food then you have to stay for the dancing," Kee said inching closer to her.

Tracie was intrigued and for the moment Jody was out of her mind. "Sure, why the hell not. You didn't ask me if I thought you were gay.?"

"I didn't ask because I didn't care if you thought I was gay or not. I am just me and that's who I want you to get to know." She touched Tracie's hand.

Tracie moved it pretending that she had to get her phone out of her bag. "I'm starved, let's eat."

Kee ordered two shots of tequila "After this."

Tracie drank half the shot in one gulp. It felt good going down her throat and warming her stomach. Kee gulped her drink down and it burned all the way down. "You haven't finished your drink."

"I think you're trying to get me drunk," Tracie said.

"What if I am? Then you'd have an excuse for anything that happens."

"Where's all this coming from? I mean we've only worked together for a couple of months," Tracie said, still not mentioning she was involved.

Kee said "I'm not one to play around when I see something I want. Let's get a table so we can have some privacy."

Kee led the way to a table in the corner with just a lit candle for light. The other tables were filling up for dinner. The waitress came over and instead of ordering food, Kee ordered more tequila.

She sat back on one side of the booth so she could see Tracie's face in the candle. "Do you believe in love at first sight?"

"What?" Tracie asked not liking what was happening.

"Love at first sight. Have you ever just met someone and said wow?" "Maybe," Tracie said still not mentioning Jody.

"Well, the first day I saw you walk in the gym I said wow." She gulped down the tequila the waitress had just put down.

"You need to take it easy with that stuff. What kind of tequila is this anyway?" Tracie said trying to change the subject.

"Patron," Kee said reaching for Tracie's hand again.

"That's good tequila. It doesn't give you a hangover," Tracie said moving her hand off the table to play with her phone.

"Do I make you nervous?"

"That's only a physical thing, that wow you keep talking about. You don't know anything about me, and I don't know anything about you," Tracie said signaling for the waitress. This time when the waitress came over Tracie ordered food for the both of them before Kee could order another drink.

"I want to get to know you." Kee said.

"What is it you want to know? "Tracie asked.

"Anything you want to tell me."

Again, Tracie changed the subject. "How you like our school?"

They both got quiet waiting for the other person to talk.

The waitress came with two plates of fried shrimp and fries and two cokes. Tracie was glad for the food. She was starting to feel intoxicated.

The band started to play, and people were leaving their tables to dance.

"Let's dance," Kee said.

Tracie looked down at her plate, but the alcohol had intensified the longing she had for a woman. "Sure."

They were the same height, so it was easy to look directly into each other eyes. They were holding each other tightly and moving only enough to keep the beat of the music.

"I'm sorry. I gotta go." Tracie said whispering in Kee's ear. The effects of the alcohol and the feeling of loneliness made her feel something for Kee that she didn't want to. She knew that something could happen that she'd be sorry for later.

"Don't go. Stay with me tonight. You won't be sorry," Kee whispered back.

"Yes, I will," Tracie said as she left Kee on the dance floor and retrieved her things from the booth.

It was a cold blast of air that hit Tracie in the face when she opened the door marked exit.

She had to walk three blocks to get her car. The cold air helped to sober her drunken brain. What was I doing? She asked herself as she stuck her hands deep in her pockets and took long strides to her car. She had to get a hold of herself before something happened that she would regret.

# Thanksgiving

Diane got up early. She wanted to make every dish that Jody liked. She was cooking turkey, yams with marshmallows, mac 'n' cheese, collard greens, homemade bread and banana pudding. She wanted this meal to be perfect; she hadn't had Jody visit her for Thanksgiving dinner since her involvement with Tracie.

She heard Jody coming down the hall and she smiled from cheek to cheek.

"What's that I smell?" Jody asked. "It smells so good."

"It's our Thanksgiving meal. Here, I made fresh bread. Have a piece with your coffee."

"You shouldn't have done all this, but I'm glad you did," Jody said with a big smile. She got quiet for a minute.

Diane noticed the change in her facial expression. "You okay?"

"Yeah, I just remembered the Thanksgivings you and I had after dad died. How much fun we had eating and watching old movies on television until we fell asleep."

"That's so good, Baby. You know then that I'm your mother."

"Yes, mom," Jody said with a big smile. She got up and gave her mother a big hug.

The spent the day just like Jody remembered, eating and watching movies until they fell asleep.

****

Gail got up early to start her part of the Thanksgiving dinner. She was tasked with the turkey and sweet potato pies. Tracie soon followed to prepare the mashed potatoes, gravy, and green bean casserole. Cooking brought back memories of the previous Thanksgiving when she and Jody were be cooking and stealing kisses in between. She heard Sam heading to the living room to watch the Thanksgiving Day parade on television.

"Sis, we got it going on in here, if I must say so myself." Gail said, sneaking a piece of one of the cooked sweet potato pies.

"I have to agree. It does smell good in here and the food looks so good I can't wait to eat," Tracie said, taking a piece of pie.

"You can't have pie for breakfast," Gail kidded with her.

"I don't see why not when I just saw you try to sneak a piece," Tracie laughed

"Mommy, Auntie Gail the parade come see. Hurry, you're going to miss Snoopy."

Gail and Tracie ran into the living room just in time to see Snoopy. They all sat and watched the parade then got ready for dinner.

"Mommy, is mommy Jody and grandma eating Thanksgiving food too?" Sam asked

Tracie felt a lump in her throat. "I'm sure they are. The last time I saw mommy Jody she said that she was going to miss you a whole bunch, but the doctor still doesn't think she's ready to come home."

"When can she come home? She's been gone a long time."

"Soon. Let's watch movies and eat pie until we feel like we're going to bust," Tracie said, trying to lighten the mood.

"I'm ready for that." Gail said.

They got up from table and headed to watch television. They spent the rest of their day laughing and eating.

# Jody and Shawn

Jody was sitting at her desk, deep in thought, when Shawn came by with an offer of dinner, which she accepted. Jody was thinking about the rumors going around the office about her. She was hurt and disgusted that people at work, then Sandy, insinuated that she was gay. She shouldn't have cared, but in honesty it did bother her. She thought it was wrong for two women to be together, but there was something that prevented her from totally denying it. It was after Thanksgiving and not much was going on. Sandy called to see if there was any progress in the case because she was tired of hiding from the media. The accusation, until now, had been semi-quiet; now it was front page news. Sandy hinted that she was thinking about taking Troy and going to see her mother in Canada. Karen said she didn't believe she'd risk everything and run. Sandy would end up in jail if she decided to try and take Troy and run. Karen and Jody sat on the couch going over the case for a little longer. When Karen left, Mr. Kincaid came in to tell her that Karen had been giving her glowing reports on her job. He wanted her to ease on to Karen's team, not standing in front of a judge yet, but become more involved than she was When Jody left the office, she had forgotten all about the thoughts that had bothered her earlier.

She was a lawyer again and that made her day. Her life was not all put together but as far as she was concerned it was getting there. She'd have to put that in the journal.

When she got home there was a note from Diane saying she had gone to Atlantic City and was staying overnight. Diane had signed the letter *Mom*. Jody smirked at the thought of her mother going to Atlantic City to get her groove on. "Go Mom, do your thing." Then she stopped smirking and looked at the clock on the wall. She had better get ready for her date. Awhile later, there was a knock at the door.

"Hey baby, you look beautiful as always," Shawn said, looking into her eyes.

"Hey. What have you got there?" she asked curiously.

"Well, do you remember our first date in your office?" he asked slyly.

She nodded.

"Okay. Then let me escort you to that limo parked out there, but you must keep your eyes closed until I say so."

She couldn't imagine what this was all about. "Remember, I don't like surprises."

"You know what, that's too bad," Shawn said, laughing. "Just go along with me on this, please."

Shawn helped her into the limo. It stopped after what she thought was a forty to fifty-minute ride. Shawn said she could open her eyes. He had taken her back to his apartment. He could see the apprehension on her face. "Shhh," he said.

They rode up in the elevator not saying any words, just holding hands. When the elevator stopped, he swept her up in his arms and carried her down the hall. He managed to get his key out his pocket and opened the door. There were roses everywhere and a small round table by the window with two covered plates on it. The view was of the Hudson River with the New York skyline as the backdrop. She was in awe of each room with roses everywhere. The music was soft, and the lights dim. Shawn took her hands after putting her on the floor. They started dancing slow to the background music.

"These have been the best days of my life," he said. "I can't imagine anything more wonderful. I know you have a long way to go, but I'm here for you now and always." She held him closer and could feel his erection on her thigh. "Shawn, you've been amazing."

He cupped her chin, raised her head and kissed her gently. His touch was so soft that she almost didn't realize what was happening.

"Jody, I have wanted you for so long. I've always been in love with you. I know no one believes in love at first sight, but it's real. It's real because it happened to me the first time I saw you. I've waited for this moment for the last five years." The look of love and caring he had on his face stirred something in her.

She took his hand and led them into the bedroom. She started undressing him.

"Jody, are you sure?" he asked.

"Very," she said.

She unbuttoned his shirt and kissed his nipples. He moaned under her touch. He unbuttoned her blouse and with one hand released her breasts from the constraints of her bra. He kissed them so gently that Jody couldn't help but moan with pleasure. He laid her on the king-sized bed and removed her pants and panties. She unbuttoned his pants as he kneeled over her. She took out his penis and held it with one hand and masturbated herself with the other. She was

about to come when he took both her hands and placed them above her head. He then placed his penis in her center and rubbed it up and down. He tried to entered her and she screamed.

"What's wrong? Did I do something wrong?" Shawn jumped up afraid he hurt her.

"No, Shawn I'm ok. She said as she pulled away from him. Maybe I'm not as ready as I thought." She was embarrassed. He laid back down next to her.

Finally, Shawn said, "Let's eat."

"That sounds good," she said with forced enthusiasm. She didn't feel like eating, but she knew he went to a lot of trouble to make this special. "You know whatever is on that plate is cold."

"No, it's not," he said with a smirk. "I'll bet you five dollars."

"You're on," she said.

They both dressed and went into the living room. The music was still playing. They lifted the lids at the same time, and nothing was there. "You had this planned," she laughed

"No, I was hoping... let's order," he said.

# The Apology

There was a note on her desk saying Kee had the flu and wouldn't be in. Tracie figured like her, Kee was embarrassed. Tracie thought she'd be the bigger person and break the ice.

She went to the registrar's office to get her number. The phone rang and rang then the answering machine picked up.

"Kee, its Tracie. If you're there, pick up." No voice came to the other end. "I just want you to know there's no hard feeling about the other night. We both had too much to drink. Everything is cool with us, I hope. I hope you feel better. Bye." Tracie sat down.

The phone rang about twenty minutes later.

"Hello."

"Hey Tracie, Its Kee. Thank you for calling and saying what you said. I'm sorry for how I acted."

"No problem, we both had too much to drink. It's forgotten," Tracie said, trying to make this as easy as possible for them both.

"I did mean some of the things I said. I just came on too strong with the alcohol. Can I ask you a question?"

Tracie didn't know how to respond. She was quiet for a minute. "I guess."

"I know we've been out together only a couple of times and we've worked together 2 or 3 months. I like you. I really would like to get to know you better if that's possible."

Tracie was shocked. She didn't know how to answer. She didn't say anything for a minute because she wanted to say the right thing. She had to be honest with herself. If she wasn't married, she'd probably say hell yes to Kee, but she was married, and she loved Jody more than life itself. She had to be honest. "Kee from what I know about you and what I see I wish I could say yes, but I'm married. I love my spouse and I'm sorry if I gave you the wrong impression. I would be a dog if I played with your feelings knowing I would never leave my spouse."

Kee was silent for a minute. "No, I'm sorry. I just assumed since you lived with your sister and you never mentioned anyone else but your daughter, that you were available."

"My spouse and I are going through something right now. Again, I'm sorry for not making things clearer."

"It's okay, I'm glad you're being honest. See you tomorrow. Bye." Kee said with disappointment in her voice.

Kee hung up before Tracie could say another word.

Tracie felt bad but she was glad everything was out.

***

Sam was in the tub which meant the bathroom was off limits for at least forty minutes. Sam didn't take two toys with her to bath she took what seemed like an entire toy store. Tracie peeked in on her and threw her a kiss. Sam threw a kiss back.

"I miss Mommy Jody."

"Me too, Sam. I hope it won't be too much longer."

"Me too," Sam said pushing a boat with her toes.

Tracie walked away. She hated having to lie. Sam was starting to ask for Jody more often. Tracie walked into kitchen where Gail was preparing a snack. "Sis, you're never gonna believe what happened today. I got hit on by my co-worker.

Gail smirked. "I know you think every woman wants you but your co-worker."

"Very funny. The other evening, we had dinner at this gay bar." Tracie said sitting down.

"Whoa, you mean you've been tipping out on Jody?" She pulled up a seat with her tea and sandwich.

Tracie didn't think she needed to tell Gail the whole truth. She left out a few details. "Are you crazy?" Tracie said. "I just needed to clear my head, so I agreed to go. Besides, teachers go for drinks together all the time."

In between chews of her pastrami on rye Gail said, "Hey, don't get so serious. I was only kidding."

Tracie reached over to take a bite of Gail's sandwich. "Sorry, Anyway, the other night at the club she gets drunk and tries to get me drunk. She starts acting like some horny teenager. Only I came to my senses before things went too far.

"Trace, you got a book going on here. Keep her around for added chapters." Gail almost choked on her food from laughter.

Tracie got up when she heard Sam coming out the bathroom. "Thanks. You're a big help. If there's a spot on the Tonight Show for a comedian, they should hire you."

"I'm sorry, but it's funny knowing how you feel about Jody. I'm surprised she got that far."

"It's going to be very uncomfortable at work," Tracie said seriously.

"This is true." Gail took another bite of her sandwich. "I wouldn't worry too much about it. I'm sure she will get over you."

"I hope you're right," Tracie said as she met Sam in the hallway. "Hey munchkin."

"Hi mommy. You hope Auntie Gail's right about what?"

"Nothing for you to worry your pretty head about. How about a game of dominoes before bed?" Tracie asked.

"Yes!" screamed Sam.

"You go and put your pajamas on, and I'll meet you in the kitchen." Sam ran to her room.

Tracie returned to the kitchen. Gail was watching her closely

"You like her, don't you?"

"Gail, that's not the point I'm happily married. I just need my spouse to realize it."

"You better keep her number just in case." Gail said, still ribbing her.

"Just in case what, Gail? Jody will come to her senses."

"How long are you willing to wait?"

"As long as I feel there's a strand of hope I'll wait. It's not just me, Gail, there's that little girl in there."

"Hey, lighten up. I was just teasing. I know how you feel about Jody."

Sam came running full steam ahead down the hall. "Dominoes time."

Tracie picked her up and snuggled the fresh clean scent of soap.

# Shawn's Surprise

Shawn was waiting for Jody when she arrived at work. "I need to see you this evening." "Can it wait? I was thinking about a book and a long bubble bath tonight." She shifted her briefcase to the other hand.

"It could, but I don't want it to. I'm too excited. Let me make dinner for you. No funny business." He gave her his most sexy smile.

"Okay, but let's make it early. I want to be here when the investigator interviews a client. I forgot to tell you my big news. Kincaid came by yesterday to tell me that he thinks I'm ready to sit in on a case. I don't have to sit on the sidelines anymore. I feel like an almost lawyer again."

"Well, then, we have a lot to celebrate. Why don't you just come over after work?" "What? No limo? Ah shucks." Jody laughed.

"You ain't said nothing but a sentence. The limo will be here when you get off." Shawn gave her a *you can't get nothing past me* look.

"Then I'll see you tonight," Jody said as she touched his arm.

When Jody got to her office, she placed a call to her mother to let her know she wouldn't be home for dinner. After that, Karen called to say she had the flu and wouldn't be in. The day was pretty boring, leaving Jody to her thoughts to fill the day. Jody made up her mind that she'd try again with Shawn at what they started the other night. She attributed the pain of Shawn trying to enter her from the accident. How? She didn't have a clue, but tonight would be different. The limo was waiting when she came out of the building. There was champagne, roses and chocolate for her to nibble on during the ride. She started to read the paper and by time she reached the sports section, she was there. Shawn was downstairs to meet her. She figured the limo driver must have called him along the way. He kissed her as soon as she had two feet planted outside the car. They held hands as they rode up in the elevator. The door to his apartment was open, with soft music filling the hall. The table was set with two plates for dinner.

Shawn turned her around from the window she was looking out.

"Is something wrong?" he asked.

"No. Shawn, I know this may be bold but make love to me right here in front of the window."

Shawn pulled her into him and kissed her long and hard. He unbuttoned her blouse and kissed her nipples through her bra. She moaned. He started to unzip his pants, but she stopped him with her hand. She continued to unzip him and pull his penis from his pants. He reached under her skirt to discover that she had on no underwear. He lifted her off the floor and tried to enter her. She screamed.

"I'm soo sorry, baby," Shawn said, jumping back from her.

Jody fixed her skirt and buttoned her blouse.

"We could try again with some lubricant," Shawn said still erect.

"No, I think I want to go home. I'm just not hungry. I'm sorry," she said.

"You don't have to go. We can still eat," Shawn said as he tucked his penis back in his pants.

"No, maybe some other time," Jody said.

"Are you sure? Because I make a mean cordon bleu. It's ham and melted cheese on top of a fried chicken breast. Yummy, yummy," Shawn said, trying to lighten the mood. "By the way, where were your panties?" he laughed.

She had to laugh with him. "I took them off at work, knowing I was going to see you tonight." Then she got serious. "The meal you're going to cook sounds delicious, but I'm just not hungry.

Really."

"Listen, you aren't doing anything to me. It'll happen. As much as you want me, I want you. I want your body to want me as much as your mind. You're not a virgin, are you? I mean, am I the first?" Shawn said walking toward her.

"Shawn, I do want you. I don't know what the problem is. I mean, I'm a grown woman. I assume I've had sex before. I really don't remember what my sex life was like. I hate to think I had a problem with sex."

"We'll deal with whatever the problem might be. Why don't you stay with me tonight?" he asked with dreamy eyes.

"Not this time," she said firmly. Shawn reached in his pocket and went down to one knee "Well, then I have one more surprise for the evening before I take you home. I know it may be too soon for you, but for me I know it's right. Please be my wife?" Shaw looked at her with pleading eyes

Jody was almost speechless. "What can I say... I can't. I have a lot to remember, and it wouldn't be fair to you."

Shawn took the five-carat diamond engagement ring from its box. "I'm only asking that you wear this ring with the intent to one day be my wife. It doesn't have to be next month or even next year but when you are ready."

"Shawn, how can I say no when you put it like that? I would love one day to be your wife," Jody said, ignoring the fact that she was supposed to be married. She knew what the doctors said but refused to acknowledge that was real.

Shawn put the ring on her finger and gave her a long, deep kiss. Then he left the room with a big grin, yetshe left the room feeling like something wasn't right.

He was good to her, but she seemed to not be able to give him the full commitment he wanted. Maybe taking his ring would make up for some it. He was so elated on the ride home that he didn't notice she hadn't said a word.

When she got home, she took off the ring before her mother could see it. She didn't want to answer any questions.

Jody called Tracie when she was alone in her room. It was time for her to find out about their relationship She wanted to move ahead with her life.

Tracie answered the phone. "Hello?"

"Tracie, it's Jody," Jody whispered.

"Hey, is everything alright?"

"Yeah, everything is fine. Are we still taking Sam to the Children's Museum?" Jody asked.

"Yep, I was going to call you to make sure we were still on, but I'm glad you called me." Tracie was ecstatic.

"Okay, see you this weekend." She hung up before Tracie had a chance to say anything else.

Sam and Tracie met Jody at the Children's Museum at eleven. Tracie was nervous, almost sick to her stomach. She held Sam's hand and had explained to her that mommy Jody was still sick so she might act a little funny. She should just enjoy spending time with her. She knew it was hard for a young child to understand, but Sam had nodded as if she understood. Tracie spotted Jody standing just inside the entrance of the museum. She was wearing tight jeans and a sweatshirt pulled down over her butt. It took Jody a minute to move in her direction. She was in awe of her body.

"Hey, Tracie," she greeted them and then looked down at Sam. "You must be Sam."

Sam nodded her head and said, "Of course I am. Are you coming home soon?"

"Sam," Tracie whispered. "Remember, Mommy Jody is still sick and there are a lot of things she doesn't remember right now. Remember what I told you. Let's just have fun, okay?"

Sam nodded.

"Let's hit the finger-painting table before lunch," Tracie said, hoping to put smiles on all their faces.

Jody made a swooping noise toward Sam. Sam pretended to be frightened. They all had a big laugh.

"Where do you live now?" Sam asked Jody quizzically.

Jody looked at Tracie. "With Diane. How's school? Do you remember your pencils when you

pack your book bag?" Jody didn't know why she said anything about Sam's packing her book bag.

Tracie was speechless at what she just heard. They were both glad Sam spoke.

"Yes, they are in my book bag at Auntie Gail's," Sam said. "

They went from activity to activity, letting Sam have fun. Sam said her stomach was hungry, so they decided to stop and eat. They all had burgers, fries and Cokes. They were all enjoying the day laughing and giggling at what Sam did. This was how it was before the accident, a lot of love between the three of them.

Tracie wished this day never had to end.

When the day was over Sam gave Jody a big kiss. Then she took Tracie's hand and placed it inside Jody's and smiled. Jody looked ashen and abruptly dropped Tracie's hand and made an excuse about having to go to the bathroom. When she returned, Tracie apologized.

"I'm sorry about that. Sam is just remembering how it was and I'm sorry if that bothered you."

"No problem," Jody said. But she still seemed unnerved.

Jody had come by bus, so Tracie gave her a ride home. Sam fell asleep in the back seat as soon as she sat down. When they reached Ms. Jones's house, Tracie was so caught up in the day that she leaned in toward Jody for a kiss. But then she realized what she was about to do and pulled back, heartaching.

Jody stared at her in silence for a moment. "Thank you for the day."

"No problem," Tracie said, trying to think of something to make the time last a little longer. "Wait, let me take you out Saturday to show my appreciation for being so understanding." "That's not necessary," Jody said with her hand on the door handle.

Tracie looked into her eyes hoping to see the Jody she knew. "I know, but you've been such a sport about the day. I really would like to show my appreciation. Please," Tracie pleaded.

"Okay," Jody said and opened the door to climb out. She saw her mother heading down the walkway.

"Hello Tracie," Diane said, standing next to Jody.

"Hey, Ms. Jones."

Diane looked in the back and saw Sam sleeping. "She has gotten so big since the last time I saw her."

"Yeah, It's been a while."

"We had a good time today at the museum. When she sat down in the car she went out like a light," Jody said, wanting to get her mother inside.

"I just wanted to come out and see her. Tell her I love her. Drive carefully. Goodnight."

Tracie started the car "Goodnight. See you Jody."

"Goodnight."

***

Gail, however, couldn't wait to find out everything. "How did it go?"

"It went great, really good, and guess who came out to see Sam?" Tracie said, smiling.

"Who?" Gail asked excitedly.

"Ms. Jones. I don't know what's going on with her being all nice to me, but I'll take it." Tracie said still smiling.

"What's that smile for? I know something good must have happened. I haven't seen you smile like that about Jody in months."

"She agreed to go out with me again," Tracie said, smiling some more.

"That's great. Does that mean she's changed back to the old Jody?" Gail asked.

Tracie grew sad. "No, she isn't the old Jody."

Gail went over to comfort her sister. "How'd she act with Sam?"

Tracie sat down and slumped in a chair. "Just like the old Jody. They laughed and hugged. Jody even said the same thing about Sam packing her pencils."

Gail sat in the chair next to her. "At least you have some hope."
"Hope? How'd you come to that conclusion?" Tracie asked.

"Because she didn't leave, curse or say anything upsetting to Sam," Gail said obviously trying to be positive.

"Yeah, that's true. I'll take hope anyway I can," Tracie said. "Goodnight." "Goodnight," Gail said.

***

Jody told her mother she was going to the museum with Tracie and Sam. She didn't understand why her mother seemed alarmed.

"How'd it go?" Now it was just the two of them.

"Like I said outside, we had a good time" Jody said hanging up her jacket.

"So, everything went alright?" Diane asked again.

"Everything went great. Now go to bed. Goodnight." Jody walked off toward her room.

ANITA POWELL

# The Case

Karen got right to the point when Jody walked into her office.

"We got problems," she said, annoyed.

"What's going on?" Jody set her purse down on her desk.

"It's Margo. She called to tell me to keep that bitch Sandy away from her house or she'd have her locked up for trespassing," Karen said

"What? I don't understand," Jody said.

"It seems Sandy showed up at their son's school and took him for ice cream after school. She didn't let Margo know, so Margo was in a panic thinking he was kidnapped."

"Maybe she's just blowing off some steam," Jody tried to reason.

"I don't think so. You should have heard her. I am sick and tired of trying to get through Sandy's head that she can't see him," Karen said, "I don't know what else to do."

Jody sat down and thought about this situation. She felt she needed to do something for the child's sake, but she didn't understand why her feelings were so strong. "Let me try. Have her meet me in the conference room at ten."

"Okay, good luck. I gotta client I have to see," Karen said as she left her office.

The receptionist called to say Sandy was being escorted to the conference room at exactly ten. Jody gathered her thoughts as well as her things and headed down the hall. They met at the door.

Sandy smiled. "You wanted to see me?"

"Yes, please come in and have a seat." Jody directed her to the far end of the table. She sat across from her.

"I asked to see you because I'd hate to see you hurt your case because you did something stupid."

Sandy was confused. "What are you talking about?"

"Margo called this morning and told Karen all about the afterschool ice cream run."

Sandy looked at Jody. "I only wanted to see my kid."

"I understand that, but do you want to go to jail? Do you think a judge is going to be quite so understanding? A judge is going to think you can't take orders and you can't stay away from children even if it's your own child."

"You know it's not like that. I just miss him."

"Yes, I know, but a judge won't care about your reasons. He's just going to put you in jail. Do you understand?" Jody asked.

"Why'd Karen send you to deal with me?" Sandy asked.

Jody cleared her throat "Karen didn't send me. I asked to come."

"Really. Why? I got the feeling you didn't like me anymore than Karen."

"I can't speak for Karen, even though I don't think she has a problem with you except

you staying away from Troy. I can tell you that I don't have a problem with you. If I did, I wouldn't be here now."

"Does that mean you're pro-gay?" Sandy asked.

"It doesn't mean I'm pro anything. What it means is I hate to see a woman go to jail for being stupid," Jody said, again clearing her throat.

"Well, for you, I'll will try to do as I've been told. But when this is over and I'm cleared,

I want you to represent me in getting my son back."

"Let's get you cleared first," Jody said, gathering her things.

Sandy stood and headed for the door. She turned to face Jody. "I'm not kidding. I want my

son and I want you to get him for me. There's one other thing... I would like to take you on a

date when this is over. To dinner. To say thanks."

Sandy left the office before Jody could open her mouth to reply. She stood shocked.

Another woman had asked her out. She couldn't figure out why. She could call Dr. Stable and tell her what's going on? But she felt embarrassed. How could she be gay when she didn't feel gay?

# Kee

When she went to work the next day, Tracie was startled to see through the office window Kee pouring coffee into two mugs. Tracie figured the best way to handle the situation was by taking her lead.

Kee heard the door open just as she took a sip of coffee. "Hey."

"Hey to you," Tracie said, taking the coffee Kee handed her.

Kee took a seat. "I want to apologize again for how I behaved the last time I saw you. Alcohol will make you say and do crazy things."

Tracie took a sip of coffee. "No problem; shit happens. We've all had one too many before."

In a quiet voice Kee said, "Yeah, but I made a total fool of myself. How can you ever respect me after that?"

Tracie took another sip of coffee. "No one was hurt, so let's just let it go." "Only if you'll have lunch with me today," Kee said looking down at the floor.

Tracie was scared to answer. She didn't want to give her the wrong impression by saying yes, and if she said no would that make it seem like all wasn't forgotten? "I have an errand to run at lunch-time; how about I run my errand and bring back sandwiches?"

Kee seemed humble. "Sure, that's okay. I have a lot of paperwork I need to catch up on anyway."

At lunchtime, Tracie brought back sandwiches and they sat quietly eating for a few

minutes. The silence was deafening to Tracie. She wanted to say something, but what?

"Did you have any problems with any of the paperwork?" Tracie asked.

Kee stopped chewing. "No, but thanks for asking. And I want you to know I appreciate you putting the other night behind us so we can still work together."

Tracie took another bite of sandwich and looked at the clock. "No problem, but I think our relationship should be purely work based."

"Sure, no problem." Kee got up and threw the rest of her sandwich in the garbage and walked right out the door to the gym floor.

There was a knock at the door. It was Lynn from the principal's office.

"Hey girl, How's it going? I been out sick so I'm just making the rounds letting everyone know I'm back."

"It's good to have you back. So, what's going on?'

"I just wanted to let Ms. Jordan know that she'll be heading to Xavier in a few weeks."

"I know she'll be happy about that. She was just out on the floor checking the equipment closet."

"Okay. Check you later."

Lynn left to find Ms. Jordan. A few minutes later Ms. Jordan came back into the office.

"I guess you heard."

"Yeah, Lynn told me when she came in looking for you."

"I think I'll take off a few weeks to get my head straight before I have to start."

"Yeah, that's probably a good idea. This might be the only time you can take off for a while. Look Kee, Ms. Jordan. I'm sorry about what happened. If I wasn't married believe me, I wouldn't mind getting to know you. I hope we can be friends. I enjoyed working with you."

"Yeah, sure, we can be friends. I'm going to put in my leave to start now." Ms. Jorden said dejected. "Bye"

Tracie felt bad but what could she do. She only wanted Jody.

# DECEMBER 2016

# Another Date

Tracie had asked Jody to meet her at Slow Dance the following Saturday after the zoo. When the Saturday arrived for their date, Tracie was a bundle of nerves about seeing Jody. They were going to meet at a gay bar; she wanted to see how Jody would act. She felt a little hope after their outing at the museum.

Tracie was standing at the bar surrounded by women ordering drinks when she saw her come in. She was wearing a turtleneck, jeans and knee-hi boots with her jeans tucked in.

"I'll take a Long Island iced tea," Jody said. "And why didn't you tell me this was an all-women's club?"

"Hello to you too, and here's your Long Island iced tea. I ordered when I saw you bulldozing your way through the crowd. And I didn't tell you because you wouldn't have given the place a chance." Tracie said.

Jody rolled her eyes and took her drink. "I have nothing against women being with women. I just don't think I had that type of relationship, nor do I want one now. That's all."

"Well, you don't mind staying for a minute, do you? Or are you scared?" Tracie asked with a grin.

"Hell, no. I'm not scared," Jody said with defiance.

That was the Jody Tracie knew, never backing down from a dare.

Just then someone bumped Jody from behind and she was forced into Tracie's arms. The smell of her aroused Tracie's clit and it started to jump. She ordered another cognac to try and control it.

"Let's dance," Tracie said. "Or did you forget how?"

"Let's do this," Jody said as Tracie grasped her hand and led her to the dance floor. Mary J. Blige had the club jumping. They danced to her and then to two more songs before Luther Vandross came on—one of Jody's favorite performers. Tracie pulled her close. Yes, she had planned this entire evening. She wanted her woman back and she was tired of feeling sorry for herself. She was ready to fight and even if she lost, at least she would go down fighting.

They slow danced to the song as if no one was in the club. Jody's body had tensed in the beginning but relaxed as the music continued to play. Tracie had expected her to run from the dance floor, but she enveloped herself in Tracie's arms. It was heaven. She held Jody so close to her that she could feel the heat from her body. Tracie reached to kiss her, getting carried away by the mood, but Jody turned her head, and she got her cheek instead of her lips.

"Trace, I think I should go. I think that drink is getting to me." She looked at her with the same want that Tracie felt.

Tracie looked into her eyes. "You called me Trace."

Jody seemed to search for words. "It just came out. Can we please go?"

"If you want." She took Jody's hand and led her out into the cool night air. "Do you want something to eat?"

Jody looked at her with uncertainty. "Yes. No. I think I should go home. I have to meet Shawn tomorrow morning. Thank you, I had a good time. It was interesting." She nervously wet her lips.

Tracie looked at her with desire. She had gotten more from her in those few hours than she had in what seemed liked years.

She knew the night was not going to end with them at home making mad love. But she would take what she could get and be grateful.

Tracie insisted on driving Jody home since she had taken the bus. When they arrived at Ms. Jones house, they sat in the car for a few minutes enjoying the Luther CD playing.

"How's it going with her?" Tracie asked.

"Good. I mean no big memory bursts, but little ones. She gives me space and answers my questions when I ask."

"That's good. I hope we can do this again sometime. I mean, as you can see, us gays aren't all bad," Tracie said with a smile.

"Sure, why not. Look, I better get in." She squeezed Tracie's hand as she opened the car door. She was gone in a flash, leaving behind her scent and memories of the evening. Tracie's desire was so strong that it felt like her clothes were cutting off oxygen to every part of her body. She needed to be alone. She went home to their apartment. When she arrived, she rushed to the bedroom and took off all her cloths and got between the cold sheets. She felt her own wetness and closed her eyes to Jody calling her name. She massaged her nipples until they were erect, and she imagined them pushed against Jody's at the club. Then she reached into the nightstand and found the vibrator and gently inserted into her vagina. She eased it in and out while she thought of the many times, they had used that very same vibrator on each other. She cried out Jody's name as her vagina tightened its grip and she came like a force of water. Then, almost at once, a calming feeling eased over her and she pulled up the covers and went to sleep

# A Reality Check

When Jody entered the house, her mother was lying on the couch.

"Hey, what you doing up so late?" Jody asked

"Waiting for you," she said. "Well, did you have a good time?

"Yeah, I did," Jody said. "You know these outings with Tracie have seemed so natural.

I mean comfortable." She fumbled to find the right words. "I mean she's okay. Not the nut I thought in the hospital. But don't get me wrong. Whatever her lifestyle is... it's not for me. Sam's a great kid and the gay club was nothing like I expected. If I had known where I was going to meet her, I probably wouldn't have gone. The thought of women being together was scary to me, but once I got there and saw what it was like the scary feeling disappeared."

"What did you expect?" her mother asked.

"That's just it. I don't know what I expected."

Jody was ready to change the subject. "I've got to show you something." She went to her room and returned. She held out her finger with Shawn's ring on it. "What do you think?"

Her mother almost gagged. "What are you thinking? You got to get things straightened out before you can marry anybody. You might not want to hear this, but you're married."

"One day I do plan on marrying Shawn. He's willing to wait until I finish sorting things out. I don't know what's going on, but I would never marry a woman. You said the Bible says its wrong, so I know I wouldn't do it." She started to get mad.

"Jody, the Bible does say it's wrong, but you went ahead and did it anyway. I don't condone what you and Tracie were doing, but maybe things are going too fast with Shawn.

"I'm telling you that I would not marry a woman. If I did maybe it was to help Tracie out for some reason. I'll get a divorce from her if that's what it takes to be with Shawn." Jody was mad. "Goodnight."

"Goodnight."

# Richard's Ultimatum

"Hello."

"Gail, I thought I'd give you one more chance to forget about mediation and settle this thing ourselves," Richard said in a commanding voice.

"Richard, we've been over this a thousand times. The answer is NO." She suddenly realized how tired she was of him.

He decided to try another tactic by softening his tone. "I want you to have your life back. You're a young, beautiful woman and I'm sure there's someone much better than me for you. When we made the pre-nup, I never thought we'd get divorced. Do you really think that pre-nup is fair since I did all the work?"

Gail thought, *more bullshit.* "Richard, remember, you left me. I put up with a lot from you. Did you really think I didn't hear about all your women? I stayed, Richard, because I loved you and thought you'd change if I were a better wife."

"Gail, you were a good wife. It's just something that men are born with, having more than one woman. We have to fool around. I think it's a gene or something. I read it in a book somewhere. I'm sorry that I hurt you Gail, but you have to agree the pre-nup is unfair."

Gail was getting mad. "Unfair? You know what unfair is? Having people tell me my husband took the temp with him on a business trip or finding receipts in your pocket for gifts I never received. What about you getting in our bed with the smell of sex and perfume on you. That's unfair."

Richard ignored what she said, so she added, "Believe me I earned every bit of that money and more."

Richard seethed with anger; he couldn't believe Gail had talked to him like that after all he had done for her. And she had the audacity to think that she should get some of his money when all she did was sit on her ass the whole time they were married.

"Bitch, you'll never get any of my money."

Gail could tell by his voice that she had pushed his buttons. "You do whatever you want but if you try any funny business, I'll make sure you go to jail. I'm not kidding, so don't try me on this. I don't give a shit about what people think, or what you think. All I want from you is what it says on that piece of paper so save your offers. I'M NOT ACCEPTING IT." She hung up. She was so mad she threw the nearest thing to her, a glass ashtray. It flew across the room, hit the wall, then shattered into a million pieces. She felt closed in. She needed to get out. Grabbing her coat, she breezed through the door and hit the sidewalk nearly running.

# Asking For Another Date

Tracie called Jody on her way to the store to ask for another date. Jody was hesitant about seeing her. She didn't want to admit to anyone, including herself, that when they were at the club, she felt something that she never felt being with Shawn.

"Please? Just for fun. I promise I won't ask again," Tracie said.

"Ok, but this has to be the last time, especially if it's going to a gay club."

It was Saturday night and the club, as always, was packed. Tracie was standing at the bar trying to get the bartender's attention when she saw Jody out of the corner of her eye. She had on a pair of skinny jeans that accentuated every curve. The blouse she wore showed just a wink of cleavage and she had her hair pulled back into a ponytail to show off her eyes.

"Hey," Jody said as she jockeyed for a spot near her at the bar.

"Hey," Tracie said, and went back to trying to get the bartender's attention.

"Let me try." She leaned across the bar, nearly blocking the way of the bartender.

"One Long Island iced tea and one cognac straight up," Jody said.

Jody had remembered Tracie's drink. It left her feeling pleasantly surprised and good about the night.

"Let's dance." Tracie took her free hand and pulled her in close. She smelled like a freshly baked apple pie and Tracie knew she wanted to eat her.

"This feels good," Tracie said to her.

They finished their dance and ordered another round of drinks.

"I feel pretty relaxed myself," Jody said.

They stood there watching the couples on the dance floor snuggling one another. Tracie knew Jody was already buzzed and by the look of her glassy eyes, the Long Island iced teas were catching up with her.

Jody rested her hand on her lap and that's when Tracie saw something that kicked her in the gut.

"What's that?"

Jody spread her fingers so Tracie could see the large diamond ring more clearly "Shawn has asked me to marry him, and I accepted,"

Tracie jumped up from her seat. Her face got very intense.

"What the fuck, Jody? How can you marry him when you're married to me?" She signaled the barmaid for another drink. She needed one fast.

"I can marry him or anyone else without asking your permission. If I married, you for whatever reason, then I want a divorce. I am not gay."

Tracie gulped down the drink and ordered another.

Tracie turned to her. "Jody, you can't marry him. Don't you have any feelings for me?" Jody didn't say anything. She just looked at her. A slow song came on and Tracie grabbed her pulled her to the dance floor. She didn't care anymore about being nice; it wasn't getting her anywhere. She held Jody close and closed her eyes so she could remember every inch of her body. Tracie startled her by whispering in her ear, "Do you want to get out of here?"

Jody was so caught up in the music and alcohol that she couldn't resist the urges that were overpowering her. She didn't understand what was going on inside her.

Jody kissed her on the lips to answer her question. She didn't know why she had done that. Jody had a war going on inside her. There were no words spoken on the ride to the apartment. When they got inside, Tracie took her hand and led her into the bedroom where she gave her another kiss and whispered, "Let me undress you."

She took off each piece of Jody's clothing, kissing each area as the material was removed. Tracie was so wet that she was afraid she might have an orgasm just from seeing her naked. She got on her knees and licked her pubic area. Jody moaned a little and opened her legs so Tracie could lick her clitoris.

Tracie didn't want her to come yet so she stopped and laid her down on the bed. This was what Tracie had dreamt of every night they'd been apart. She wanted to make it last as long as she could. This was her Jody, the one that loved to have her mornings start with them making love. Now, Tracie only hoped that this was the beginning for them.

Jody held onto her shoulders while Tracie kissed her ears and neck. Jody kissed her in return, her body burning from the scent of her skin. A moan escaped Jody's lips and before she realized it... She couldn't believe she was touching a woman and how good it felt. She wanted to get control of her body, but she couldn't. The more she touched Tracie, the more her body wanted her.

Her mind was telling her no more but, just as the thought came to her, Tracie began to lick her more intensely moving down her entire body. Jody moaned with each soft touch of Tracie's tongue. When Tracie reached her toes, she sucked each one while running her hands gently from her vagina to her feet. Tracie got on top of her to kiss her lips.

"Mmm this feels so good," Jody whispers in her ear, "Now let me undress you."

Tracie laid on her back so Jody could undress her. Jody took off each piece slowly so she could see her body. She looked at each part hungrily. She kissed Tracie's neck, nipples and pubic area. Jody couldn't believe she was doing this. She couldn't believe how enticing Tracie was. Tracie repositioned herself atop of Jody and started to grind against her. Their centers met, wet, with grinding intensity. The feeling was incredible.

Jody held her tightly; meeting her every movement until it seemed they were one. They closed their eyes as they moved faster in excitement. They held onto one another as they both shuddered from orgasm. Jody kept her eyes closed. She needed a minute with her thoughts. She thought about how natural touching Tracie seemed. She couldn't believe how good and fulfilling she felt, unlike the pain she felt when Shawn had tried. Jody didn't like where these thoughts were taking her. There had to be another conclusion. But what? She wasn't ready to accept a woman as her spouse.

They laid there for a few minutes trying to gather their thoughts. The alcohol was beginning to wear off, but the intensity of the moment still remained.

"Wow," Tracie said reaching for her.

Jody scooted over in the bed with tears in her eyes.

"What's the matter? Didn't I please you?"

"I think I should go. It's late," Jody said, trying to unravel herself from the covers. She needed to get out of there. She couldn't believe what she had done. It was all too confusing. Tracie grabbed her arm. "Wait, what's going on here? What we did was beautiful. Why do you want to leave?"

Jody turned to her. "It happened because I had too much to drink. This doesn't change anything as far as I'm concerned. I'm still marrying Shawn."

Tracie sat up. "How can you still want to marry him after what we did?"

"Please, take me home. I can't think right now." Jody said trying to find her clothes.

"Okay," Tracie said sadly. "But I wish you'd stay the night with me."

"No! Now get dressed," Jody almost screamed. The whole situation with Tracie was getting to her. Tracie got dressed and they drove in silence. Soft jazz music filled the car as they sat outside Diane's house.

Jody had cooled off some. "I'm sorry about what happened back there." "If you're really sorry you'd come back home with me," Tracie said.

Jody turned her head towards her. "No, I can't do that."

"Why? Why can't you? It's simple, just say let's go home and I'll turn the car around.

It's that simple," Tracie said with pleading eyes.

"Tracie, you don't understand. What happened back there shouldn't have happened. I'm supposed to marry a man that I care deeply for. I don't know where what happened back there came from, so no it's not easy," Jody said getting out the car.

Tracie watched as Jody walked up the walkway and entered the dark house. She saw a light by the door come on and then the living room light. She finally drove away when she saw all the lights go off. It was too late to go to Gail's, who wasn't expecting her anyway, so she drove back home.

Tracie needed time to clear her head. Everything that had been so right a little while ago somehow turned terribly wrong. She collapsed on their bed and fell asleep inhaling Jody's lingering scent. When she came to life the next morning, her head was pounding from too many drinks, and she wondered if Jody was feeling the same way. It was early, too early to call especially after last night. She laid back on her pillow with thoughts of Jody dancing through her head. She couldn't believe that Jody, her Jody, could have feelings for anyone but her. The thoughts were painful so when sleep came again, she welcomed it. It was almost dusk when she awoke to a growling stomach. She went to the refrigerator; it was bare. She found an old Chinese menu and called for a delivery. She poured herself a drink hoping it would help get rid of what was left of her headache. It was about an hour later when the doorbell startled her from her thoughts. She ate, listening to jazz music with the television on mute. She fixed herself another drink. The hours ticked on with her drinking and thinking. Soon she was buzzing and on the road to Jody's house.

She knocked and knocked on the door. Finally, Jody came. Shawn was behind her.

"What's going on, Tracie? Jody asked

"I love you," Tracie said.

"Maybe you should go home and sleep it off," Shawn piped in.

"Maybe I should kick your ass," Tracie slurred.

Jody turned toward Shawn and put her hand on his chest. "Shawn go back and watch TV.

Let me handle this."

"You sure?" He eyed Tracie.

Jody looked at him and nodded. "Yeah."

Hesitantly, he left them alone.

"Tracie, you just can't come over here without calling." Jody said.

Tracie tried to move closer to her but stumbled instead. "I'm sorry, but I needed to see you. I miss you. You mean everything to me and Sam. Jody, I can't let you marry him. It hurts me so much to think you are planning a life without us. Jody pulled her down to sit on the porch steps. She sat down next to Tracie to try and reason with her.

Jody whispered, "I'm really sorry about last night. I really drank too much. Tracie, whatever you think we had is over. I'm going to marry Shawn. You're a nice person and Sam's a good kid. I know you'll find someone if you just give yourself a chance."

Tracie looked at Jody with red eyes full of tears. "How can you say that? Find someone else. I love you." She started to get angry. "Suppose I tell him what we did last night? Do you think he'd still marry you? DO YOU?"

Jody got up. "If you do, I will never ever speak to you again. Don't threaten me."

Tracie staggered to a stand. "I'm sorry; I just don't know what to do."

Ms. Jones arrived home before Tracie could finish what she wanted to say.

"Hey, Jody," she said. "Tracie what's going on here?"

Tracie looked up with tears in her eyes. "Jody's getting married." "I know!" Ms. Jones said eyeing Tracie suspiciously.

"She's getting married to Shawn." Tracie pointed to Jody's ring finger. "See!"

"Are you drunk?" Ms. Jones asked her. Shawn opened the door and stuck his head out.

"Everything okay, ladies?" he asked. "Hello, Ms. Jones." "Hey, Shawn, it's nice to see you. Everything is fine." Jody looked at him and nodded. Shawn closed the door.

Ms. Jones looked in Tracie's direction. "I'm going to take you home. I think you need some sleep. You can pick up your car tomorrow."

Jody looked at Tracie and touched her elbow to help her mother get her down the steps. Jody's touch sent an electrical charge through Tracie's entire body. Tracie couldn't talk so she just nodded okay and let Jody and her mother guide her to the car. When she got home the bed seemed too far and Tracie fell asleep on the couch.

The next morning when she tried to raise her head, a pain shot through it. Tracie just let her head flop back down on the pillows. She tried to remember what happened last night but there were just bits and pieces of the fool she'd made of herself. When she managed to turn her head, she felt sick on the stomach. It hit her that it was real. Jody may never sleep there again.

She turned over to go back to sleep, but she heard the telephone ringing in the background.

She stumbled to answer it.

"Hello." Tracie's voice sounded like cotton was stuffed in her mouth.

"Tracie, I hope I didn't wake you." It was Ms. Jones "I just wanted to remind you that your car is here."

"Okay, I'll pick it up later," Tracie said

"No, I want you to pick it up now, before Jody wakes up," she said coldly.

"Okay, let me just put some water on my face and grab a cab," Tracie said.

Tracie was at Ms. Jones house within thirty minutes. She must have been looking out the window waiting for her because as soon as she stepped one foot out of the cab the house door opened.

"Tracie, I need to have a word with you." she said coming outside to the curb. Ms. Jones looked at her sternly. "Please don't come to my house drunk again. I know how you feel, but you coming over here drunk is not the answer."

"I'm sorry and it won't happen again. I just didn't know what to do when I saw that ring. I felt like I was losing her for sure," Tracie said as she opened her car door to drive to Gail's. Tracie gave Ms. Jones one final look before closing the door. Tracie called her job as she drove to let them know she'd need a sick day.

Tracie drove around awhile before heading to Gail's. Gail had an early meeting with her lawyer about the meditation later that day.

# Jody's
# Unresolved Issues

While Jody dressed for work her mother made breakfast. She hadn't had a chance to talk to Jody when she came back from dropping Tracie off. Jody and Shawn had left for coffee, leaving a note on the refrigerator.

"Was Tracie, okay?" Jody asked sitting down.

"What do you think? She's in love with you and it hurts her to see you with someone else," Diane said putting breakfast down.

Jody pushed the plate away. "It bothers me to hurt someone, but what can I do?"

"There's not much, I guess, but go back to your sessions so you can try and get more of your

memory back. Maybe Dr. Stable can help move it along a little faster," her mother said, pushing

Jody's plate back in front of her.

Jody picked up her fork and pushed the food around, "Mom, I can handle this. Tracie will find someone, and I'll live happily ever after with Shawn."

Her mother poured them some coffee. "Jody, I can't tell you what to do, and believe me you being gay is not something I condone. I just don't want you to get your memory back one day and realize you don't really love Shawn."

"That won't happen," Jody said smartly.

"Okay, Ms. Smarty pants, what about your father? What about your childhood? What about all the hard work you put into school, especially law school? What about all the children you've helped? Don't you want to remember them?"

Jody got up from the table and started to leave the kitchen. "I don't know," she said quietly as she left for work.

The bus was full of people, but Jody didn't see any of them. She felt like she was being pulled in all different directions. She had been called gay by Sandy and asked out on a date. Then there were her confused feelings for Tracie. Then her decision to marry Shawn. There's a marriage that she doesn't know anything about. She wished she could just stay on this bus and ride forever, going no place in particular.

But to her dismay, the bus pulled into her stop. Shawn was there with roses in hand as she got off. He handed her the roses and tried to kiss her lips. She turned her head. He asked her what was wrong. She said nothing.

They entered the building and bought coffee from the concession. Shawn asked her to have lunch with him. She declined. He pulled her to a corner far from people. They almost dropped their coffee because of how fast and hard he was pulling her. She hoped no one saw and misunderstood. She knew time was needed to sort things out. She was emotionally overwhelmed.

"What's going on with you?" he asked through clenched teeth.

"Nothing. I just want to be in my own space today," she said wiping spilled coffee from her hand.

He calmed down. "I just wanted to make sure we were okay. It seemed like you were brushing me off."

Jody wanted to lighten the mood. "And give up my limo ride? You gotta be kidding." They both laughed as they walked to the elevator. They made a date for the next night at Shawn's. Reluctantly, Shawn let her go.

When Jody got to her office, Margo was there talking to Karen.

"You remember Jody Jones, my colleague?" Karen asked Margo.

"Yeah," Margo said turning to face Jody then quickly turning back.

"What's going on?" Jody said to no one in particular.

Karen spoke. "Margo is here because she says she's getting threatening phone calls."

"Do you recognize the voice?" Jody asked trying to help Karen.

Margo looked at Jody. "If I did, I'd be in jail for beating the shit out of them."

"Calm down. I know you're upset, but that's no way to handle it." Karen said.

"Exactly what is the caller saying?" Jody asked.

"They're saying things like pervert, child molester, wait until you get in jail. And the worst is 'think about your son.'"

"Did you call the police?" Jody asked.

"No, I thought I'd come see you," Margo said coldly.

Karen looked at Margo. "We aren't the police. You should go to them. Maybe they can catch these people."

"I don't believe in cops. I think it's better if I take Troy away from this mess. I mean everyday it's something new. Sandy's trial starts any day now and there's no telling what kind of circus it's going to be. Maybe you can give me written permission for me to take him somewhere else," Margo said.

"I can't give you permission to take Sandy's son anywhere. I can't do that." Karen not believing what she was being asked.

"I'd ask Sandy, but she has enough on her mind, and I don't want to bother her with this," Margo said.

"Well, I'm sorry. Calling the police is all the advice I can give you." Karen said.

Margo stood. "Well, I just thought I'd let you know what I'm dealing with even though you're Sandy's lawyer."

They all walked toward the door.

Jody called to Margo as she walked down the hall. "I wouldn't take him without her permission. You don't want to go to jail for kidnapping."

Margo looked at her coldly and snapped her head back around and walked quickly to the elevator. Karen and Jody both showed disgust on their faces.

"Are you thinking what I'm thinking?" Karen asked.

"Yep, she wanted to say you said she could take him if anyone asked," Jody said. "I bet there hasn't been any phone calls and if there have been, why hasn't she complained until now? Since Sandy isn't there?" Karen asked.

"You're probably right. How did Sandy get involved with her? She's a piece of work," Jody said.

"You're right about that," Karen said as she grabbed her pocketbook and headed to see another client. Jody sat down and started to read one of the briefs on the case. The report said the investigator having talked to the girl at various times is wavering in her accusation. The investigator recommended them to keep delaying the court date as long as possible so he could continue his investigation.

**

Jody started rummaging through her desk looking for an additional file when her finger grabbed the picture of Tracie, Sam and her. She stared at it for what seemed like hours before she put it back to do some work. The day dragged on before the clock on the wall showed five o'clock.

She skipped dinner and went to her room. She wanted to be alone with her thoughts.

She finally drifted off to sleep with thoughts of the night she had with Tracie. She tried to wake up, but couldn't it seemed like she was transfixed in her dream. When she was finally able to stop dreaming, she sat up in bed. She felt around for the glass of water she kept on the nightstand.

The dream seemed so real. She could feel Tracie lips on her breast and her moving down her body kissing every inch. She could smell the scent of Tracie even now that she was awake. "What the fuck is happening to me?" she whispered into the darkness. She laid back down but didn't close her eyes; she was afraid that the dream would come back.

Nothing eventful happened the next day at work. She had a date with Shawn that evening and went home to take a short nap and change. When her little alarm clock chirped seven, she went downstairs to wait for Shawn. When she got downstairs, there was a limo driver holding a sign with her name. She went over to him, and the driver told her that Shawn was waiting for her at his address. She stepped inside the large Lincoln and found caviar on toast cut into little triangles, champagne and chocolate covered strawberries. She turned on the television and closed the limo curtains to keep the sun out. She then sat back and enjoyed the ride.

Shawn was there to meet her when the limo stopped.

"Hey, beautiful. Did you enjoy your snack?"

"Yes, it was delicious and quite filling," Jody said.

"I hope you're not too full because I have something special for you," Shawn said with dreamy eyes.

"I can't wait."

"I hope you can," Shawn said pulling her into the elevator.

Jody's mind was thinking. Why don't I have that feeling I get when I'm—

Shawn covered her mouth with kisses before her thought was finished. She could feel his erection on her leg as he kissed her.

"Shawn, what if the elevator stops for someone to get on?" Jody asked pushing him back."They can catch the next one, this one's occupied," he said trying to push her against the elevator wall.

"Shawn, stop it. What's got into you?" She forcefully said.

Shawn stopped. "I just want you so badly. Look," he said pointing to his erection bulgingthrough his gym shorts.

"I'm not in the mood." Jody was furious.

They got off the elevator to soft music coming from Shawn's apartment.

When they got inside, Shawn pulled her down the hall to his bedroom as if he hadn't heard her.

"Shawn, I don't want to do this," Jody said.

"Do you mean now or ever?" He sounded upset.

"Now, that's all I can talk about," Jody said.

"Jody, I love you. I've thought about you ever since I first saw you at work. I've tried to get over this feeling but every girl I've been with doesn't measure up to what I think we can have. I know it sounds crazy. It sounds crazy saying it to you. I promised myself if I ever got a chance with you, I'd do whatever it took to make you happy. Please Jody just give me a chance. If you don't want to have sex that's fine, but I just want to show you how much I want you. We can just have dinner if that's what you want. I bought us lobster for dinner. I'll put them in the boiling water. They only take a few minutes to cook," Shawn said relenting.

Jody went to the living room to wait. She was still mad. She hardly spoke to Shawn during dinner and asked him to take her home soon after. The silence was deafening on the ride home.

"Thanks for dinner, the lobster was good," Jody said.

"I know you're still mad, but please try and look at it from my point. You're going to be my wife. I love you. What is so wrong with us being together sexually? I mean I enjoy being with you without sex, but I want to know what's it like being with you sexually too."

Jody didn't know what was wrong with it. "I am trying, Shawn. And I'm sorry if I hurt you."

"It's not about hurting me. It's about you committing to me. Do you understand?" Shawn said

softly.

"I understand. There just so much going on inside me right now that I just don't understand. I gotta go," Jodie said as she ran from the car.

Jody's mother was up when she came in.

"Is everything alright?"

"Everything is fine," Jody said as she ran to her room.

Her mother followed her. "Then why are you crying?"

"I feel everyone wants something from me I can't give." She wiped her eyes.

"Honey, that's because we all love you and want you to be happy." She put her arm around her.

"I don't know what to do."

"Whatever you do, take your time and don't rush into anything."

"I won't. Thanks for listening." Jody said kissing her cheek.

Jody's mother smiled. "Get some rest we'll talk some more in the morning."

Jody got under the covers and thought about what didn't happen with Shawn and tried to figure

out why. She fell asleep telling herself that she wasn't a lesbian.

# Gail's Surprise

When Tracie got to Gail's, she was surprised to see her. She thought Gail's meeting with her lawyer would have lasted longer.

"What are you doing here?" Tracie asked surprised. Gail broke out in a big smile. "I won. It's over." "Really?" Tracie asked tired.

"Richard has agreed to everything in the pre-nup. My lawyer called just as I was leaving. Let's break out the champagne," Gail said, giddy as a child.

"I don't understand. I thought he was hell bent on not giving you anything. Now all of a sudden, he's giving in. It doesn't make any sense." Tracie said, plopping down in the first chair she saw.

"I know, I know. It's crazy but it's over. That's all I care about," Gail said popping the champagne.

Tracie looked at her wearily "So now what?"

"We all meet tomorrow to sign some papers and I'm rich and free," Gail said, sipping her champagne.

"Just like that," Tracie said declining her glass with a wave of her hand. "Gail it's not over until he's signed."

"Stop being a stick in the mud." She nearly downed, her entire glass. "By the way, you look like hell," Gail said taking the chair next to her.

"Yeah, I feel like hell too. I made a fool out of myself over at Jody's last night. I seem to keep doing all the wrong things." She held her head. "She's planning on marrying that dude from work. He gave her a ring."

"Maybe it's time you stop doing anything and give Jody time to figure this out. This is hurting you; think how confusing it must be to be pulled in two different directions."

"I'm scared, Gail. I have loved her so long that I can't see myself not having her." Tears formed in her eyes.

Gail reached over to hug her. "Yeah, I know, but sometimes love means having to let go."

"I'm not ready to, not yet" Tracie said wiping her eyes

Gail looked her straight. "It's not just your choice, Trace, It's hers, too. It's not just you having to go on, but Sam too."

"What am I going to say to Sam?"

"You'll think of something when the time is right. Why don't you try and get some rest.

Do you need me to call your job before it gets any later?" Gail asked.

"No, I took care of that on the ride over. Did Sam say anything this morning?" Tracie asked trying to refocus herself.

"No, she just asked for you and I told her you had a late business meeting, so you stayed at your house," Gail said, "Oh, by the way, whatever happened with your co-worker?"

Tracie got up and headed to her room. "She went to a new job at another school. Goodnight or good day," Tracie said as she went to her room.

Gail had a few more glasses of champagne and laid on the couch for a nap. The clock awakened her at two-thirty to pick up Sam. The way Tracie looked, Gail figured she'd let her rest as long as she could. When Sam got home, she ran straight to her mother's room and jumped on the bed.

Sam asked her where she had been last night, and did she see Mommy Jody. Tracie wiped the sleep from her eyes. She wasn't ready to answer any questions. She told Sam the same lie Gail suggested. Sam accepted what Tracie said. Sam was just glad Tracie was home and they were together. She challenged Tracie to a monopoly game after dinner. Tracie happily agreed.

***

The next morning, Gail got ready for her meeting. She was so excited she arrived at her lawyer's office an hour early where they drank coffee and waited for Richard and his lawyer. The appointment time came and went and there was still no Richard or his lawyer. Gail's lawyer finally decided to call Richard's lawyer, and Gail could only hear faint yelling from the next room. He was furious when he came back. Richard was still going to fight the pre-nup and his lawyer hadn't bothered to call to cancel the appointment. Richard's lawyer said that in view of this recent change he would be asking the court for more time to confer with his client. Gail's lawyer countered that he would be asking the court as soon as he hung up the fucking phone to expedite this matter since it been dragging on for too long.

Gail fought tears. She was furious. Tracie was right, it was not like Richard to give in so easily. She told her lawyer to do whatever he had to. She wanted this over ASAP.

Needing to clear her head, she decided to go for a drive. She couldn't believe she let Richard make a fool out of her again. She called Tracie at work.

"You were right about Richard. He didn't show," Gail said angrily.

"I'm sorry, Gail. I tried to tell you." She sighed. "Never mind. Is there anything I can do?"

"No, nothing. I'm just going to drive around for a bit. How are you feeling this morning?"

"I'm as good as it's gonna get for a while. I've been thinking maybe it's time for Sam and I to move back home."

"You don't have to do that. You haven't come up with what you're going to say to Sam, maybe it would be better to stay for a while longer," Gail said.

Gail didn't know how to say it, but she'd miss them terribly. They had been a source of relief after dealing with Richard.

Tracie sensed that maybe Gail didn't want to be alone yet. "You might be right. We'll stay a little longer."

"I'm glad to hear that." She was relieved that she didn't have to be alone yet.

"Okay, you want me to pick up Sam since you have a lot on your mind?" Tracie asked.

"No, I'll get her. Sam has a way of making you forget your problems," Gail said with a laugh.

Tracie laughed as well and said good-bye. She went back to busying herself with work. She thought about Gail and Jody as she was making the lesson plan for next week.

# The Breakup

Jody's mother was making breakfast when Jody finally came downstairs.

"How are you this morning?" she asked, setting Jody's breakfast in front of her.

"I'm okay." Jody didn't look at her.

"You know, I didn't get much sleep last night thinking about your problems." She sat down across from Jody. Diane made sure Jody was looking at her. "I don't think you should marry Shawn. There, I said it. Please hear me out before you start to get all defensive. You don't have any memory of Tracie, but I can tell you have feelings for her. Don't tell me you don't because I can tell by the way your face lights up especially lately. Believe me, that was hard for me to say. Don't think I've changed my mind about you, but I realize that your happiness comes first. Sometimes people agree to situations, not really understanding the impact it will have on their lives later. Shawn may have agreed to wait, but Jody, how long should you put his life on hold? What I'm saying is maybe you should not accept his ring right now but wait until you have resolved your issues. If you both still want to get married after that, you can have my blessing. But not before."

Jody knew her mother was right. She had to give Shawn back his ring until she could resolve her feelings for Tracie and her other issues. She wanted to know exactly what kind of relationship she and Tracie had. She needed to know why her body responded to Tracie so readily and struggled when it came to Shawn. Jody called Shawn and they made plans to drive to the Poconos for lunch. She kept the conversation light on the drive up. When they reached the restaurant at Mt. Airy Lodge, they were seated immediately.

"Wow, this is nice." Shawn said

"Yeah, I saw it on a television commercial," Jody said with a tight smile

"Why do I get the feeling that there's more to this lunch?"

The waiter came and took their order, which gave Jody time to think. "Let's talk about it after we eat."

"Sure, whatever you want." Shawn reached for Jody's hand, the one that was playing with the saltshaker.

She pulled her hand back. They sat in silence until their food was brought out.

They ate in silence enjoying the atmosphere.

Shawn lifted his glass. "To us. And a long, happy life together. For always."

She didn't drink. "Shawn, I need to talk to you," she said with sadness in her voice.

"I guess the truth for this impromptu date will now come out," he said softly. "Jody, what's going on?"

She took off the ring and placed it in his hands.

"What's this all about?"

"Shawn, I can't put your life on hold while I figure things out or until I can remember all of what my life used to be. You're a great guy and any woman would be very lucky to have you. I know you said no pressure, but what happens if I find out I really was in love with someone else? I mean, you have never asked what I remembered about my relationships. Shawn, there is so much I still need to know. There's a whole other person that you don't know." Jody looked away, not wanting him to see the tears swell in her eyes.

Shawn turned her face so he could look her in the eyes. "I heard rumors at work that you were a lesbian and Tracie was your partner. I didn't and don't care. I love you. You losing your memory maybe was a bad thing for you, but it was like God did it just so we could be together."

"You mean you heard rumors about Tracie and me and never said anything?" she asked not sure she heard him right.

"I didn't believe or want to believe you and her were anything but friends. I just wanted you and if that means you not remembering your past, I don't care."

"Shawn, you might only care about us going off happily ever after, but I care about so much more. I had a life that was taken from me. How could I ever be totally happy in a new life until I can put my other life behind me? That means confronting it, not hiding from it."

"But do you have to give the ring back? I can wait. Really."

"Shawn, no, it won't work. Suppose I find out I can't marry you and you've wasted years waiting? You would hate me."

Shawn looked at her with tears in his eyes. "I could never hate you, Jody. I just don't understand you picking a woman over me."

"I'm not choosing anyone over anyone else. That is not what I'm saying at all. I have to know what I feel for—" She stopped, not wanting to cause any more tension.

"Feelings, feelings for whom? It surely isn't feelings for me that you're concerned about or you wouldn't be doing this. You do have feelings for her, that's why you won't commit to me." His voice lowered in anger. "What has all this been? Were you just using me the whole time?" He now had such contempt in his voice for her.

"You've got it all wrong. I still don't know anything for sure. I'm confused. My mother helped me to realize that I was in denial about some things."

Shawn jerked his hand from hers "So now it's your mother that's giving out advice. Everybody knew about your little secret except for me. I guess the rumors were true. What were you all doing? Laughing behind my back? I can't believe this." He rose to leave. "Let's go." He paid for their meal and headed for the car. Jody was walking far behind him. In the car Shawn turned the radio up loud so they would have no conversation.

"Shawn," Jody said when they reached her house. "I'm sorry. I never meant to hurt you. I hope one day you can forgive me, and we can become friends,"

"Forgive you? Just stay away from me, Jody. I'm done."

She watched him drive away and tears again welled up in her eyes but this time they fell. She had hurt him. She knew deep down that it was necessary. She also felt relief. She suddenly had this odd feeling that her life was changing.

But first things first. She had to understand the feelings she felt for Tracie. She also knew she couldn't make her any promises either.

***

The next few days at work were quiet. Karen and Jody still talked, but her friend seemed to be distant.

"What's up, Karen?" Jody asked while they were reviewing briefs one day.

"Nothing, just tired. You know how it is when you have a demanding child and an even more demanding husband." Karen seemed nervous.

"Can I help with anything?" Karen was a good friend to her, and she wanted to be one in return.

"No, I'm good. Are you okay?" she asked with concern. "I don't mean to pry, but are you okay?"

"I guess you've heard about Shawn and me," Jody said. "Karen, I can't make him understand that it didn't have to end forever, but for right now it needs to be this way. He's a good guy. I didn't want him to spend his whole life waiting for me."

"Jody, Shawn's saying you broke up with him because you wanted to be with a woman. I'm telling you this because I think it's wrong to spread rumors. His pride is obviously hurt and he's trying to mend it by sleeping with the entire sixteenth floor."

Jody was beyond mad. "Thanks for telling me."

She got up and walked with purpose down to Shawn's office. When she reached his door, she didn't bother knocking.

"Shawn, what the fuck are you doing spreading rumors about me? I thought we were both going to be grownups about this." She glared at him.

"Rumors? I thought they were facts, or are you having a memory lapse day?" His tone was cold.

"Look, Shawn, I'm sorry for what happened. This had nothing to do with anyone else. I was only trying not to ruin your life. I'm sorry you can't and won't understand that. But keep my business out of your fucking mouth."

Shawn stalked toward her. "Get the fuck out of my office."

She turned and slammed his door behind her. Then she walked quickly to the ladies room to cry. She felt she needed some time off to deal with all that was happening. She called her boss once she was back in her office. She needed time off to understand all that was going on. Jody also let him know she wouldn't be able to help Karen finish the case. Her boss assumed it had to do with her medical condition, so he approved it.

# The Restart

A few days later Tracie received an unexpected call from Jody saying she wanted to see her that evening.

They hadn't had any contact since Tracie's drunken episode. Excitement slowly began to course through her body. Maybe she'd forgiven her.

They decided to meet at another one of their favorite restaurants, The Crab and Shrimp Shack. Jody was sitting in a booth staring off into space when Tracie walked in. She looked so good sitting there in a white turtleneck and gray skirt, playing with her fingers.

Tracie, also in thought crossed the restaurant toward her. So much of their lives had been wasted because someone had fallen asleep at the wheel. Where would they be had that not happened? Would things ever be the same again?

"Hey, you," Tracie said as she slid into the opposite side of the booth.

"Hey," Jody said coming back to reality

"Are you hungry? I know I am. The crab legs here are off the hook." Tracie tried to sound upbeat but for some reason she sensed that something seemed wrong.

"Sounds good," Jody said, but she was obviously distracted. Then she blurted out,

"Shawn and I have broken up."

Tracie didn't know what to say. She didn't want the wrong words to come out.

"Okay," Tracie said slowly. "Is there anything I can do? I mean, are you okay?"

"Yeah, I'm fine but he's spreading rumors that I'm gay. Actually, he is confirming the rumors that I'm gay. I can't believe he's doing that SHIT."

Tracie was getting mad. She didn't like the fact that he was trying to hurt Jody.

She reached for her hand to comfort her. "I'm sorry. What an asshole."

Jody took back her hand and said with anger, "He actually had the nerve to tell me that he didn't care if I got my memory back. That none of the rumors mattered, that none of it mattered as long as I was with him."

"That's a man for you." It was all Tracie could come up with to say. She didn't know where this was going but she knew she had to be supportive right now.

Jody lowered her head as if she was about to tell her some mysterious secret.

"My mother made me realize I couldn't put his life on hold while I sorted my life out. I mean, Shawn was a good guy, at least I thought he was, and it wouldn't have been fair to keep him hanging on."

"Are you remembering things about your life before the accident?" Tracie asked anxiously.

"Trace, that's not what's happening exactly. I mean that's not why I've asked you here. I needed to talk, and I thought you might be a good listener. The other night at the club I got this

feeling in my body when you held me close. When I was with Shawn, I didn't get that feeling.

It's hard to explain."

"Jody, feel me on this. Why don't we go back to the beginning?"

She looked at her. "What do you mean the beginning?"

"Well, when I first saw you, it was at that club we were at the other night. Maybe going back sparked a feeling, so let's try it again this Saturday." Tracie wanted her to sense the hope in her voice.

They had been so involved in their conversation they didn't notice the steaming crab legs sitting between them.

Jody thought about what Tracie was saying. She wanted to remember what role this person sitting in front of her had in her life.

She needed to know why Tracie could make her feel what Shawn couldn't.

"Okay," she said finally seeing the crab legs sitting between them.

# Back To The Club

It was Saturday night and the club, as always, was packed. Tracie spotted Jody making her way through the crowd. She broke out in a grin, hoping that this was a new beginning for them. Jody's presence always seemed to get attention, and today was no different. She was wearing skinny jeans that accentuated her butt. With her coat open, her tight midriff shirt showed just enough skin.

"Hey," she said as she moved for an open spot near Tracie at the bar.

"Hey," Tracie said as she stopped the barmaid to get them drinks.

"Mmm, this is good." Jody said, after sipping her drink. The music started, and Tracie pulled her in close. She smelled like a freshly baked apple pie, and Tracie knew she wanted her.

Jody didn't say anything when Tracie pulled her close. She wanted to push away, but her body wouldn't move.

They finished their dance and ordered another round of drinks.

"I think two is my limit. I don't want anything to happen that I'm not fully responsible for."

"Jody, nothing will happen unless you want it to. I promise. I'm not the kind of person that would take advantage of any woman."

They stood around watching the other couples on the dance floor holding each other tightly and whispering in each other's ears.

When the lights in the club went almost completely out, it seemed like everyone was trying to find a partner. It was the last dance. Tracie took Jody's hand, not to lead her but more of a way of asking her to dance. Jody responded by closing her hand in Tracie's. They held each other tightly; no words were needed between them. When the music stopped playing, Tracie stepped backed from her.

"I want to make love to you again," she whispered.

Jody looked at her for a minute. She knew not only what her body was telling but her heart too.

*No,* she briefly thought, *I can't.* But those words didn't come out of her mouth. "Okay," Jody whispered.

Tracie took her hand and moved through the crowed dance floor to the door. The night air had a mist to it, so they ran for the car never letting go of each other. They let their hands part to get in the car. Once inside, they reconnected their hands for the drive to Tracie's. No words were spoken, or any glances stolen between them. The magic of the moment was all that was needed. When she opened the door, they didn't notice the musky air of the closed-up apartment.

Tracie kissed Jody's lips and guided her to the bedroom. They started to undress each other as soon as they entered. Tracie kissed Jody's erect nipples once she was free from her shirt and bra. Jody was craving this moment. She needed to feel Tracie's body immediately. She ripped her shirt open. The intense pleasure from Tracie kissing her nipples was driving her crazy. She practically tore Tracie's undershirt from her body. Jody sucked Tracie's nipples and put her hand between her legs. She could feel the heat coming from Tracie's vagina through her pants. She unbuckled Tracie's belt and eased her hand down into her boxers. When she eased her hand between Tracie's vagina lips, she gasped at how wet she was. Jody's heart quickened and the feel of Tracie's wetness aroused her even more.

Jodie guided her to the bed and took off her pants and began to suck on her clitoris. Tracie moaned with pleasure. She reached up and found Tracie's breasts and squeezed them lightly. Then she found her nipples that were at attention and she flicked them back with her fingers. Jody never stopped licking or gently biting Tracie's clitoris. Tracie started to move her hips in time with Jody's licking. Jody sensed that she was about to erupt. Tracie pushed Jody's face further in her vagina. Jody almost couldn't breathe because of the pressure from Tracie on her head. Then Tracie released all the built up feeling she had. Jody tasted the sweet salty cum and licked Tracie until she released her head. They lay there tired for a few minutes relishing the feeling of what just happened. Jody couldn't believe what she had just done, nor could she believe how aggressive she was doing it. She was about to say something about her feelings to Tracie when Tracie started to cover her mouth with kisses. Tracie finished undressing her. Tracie kissed her from her lips to her toes, sucking them seductively. She kissed her way back up Jody's legs to her vagina and licked her lips. Jody started pushing Tracie's head down wanting her to suck every part of her. She took one of Tracie's hands and moved it down to her vagina. She wanted her to enter her with her fingers. Jody moaned with pleasure and started moving her hips from the sensation of Tracie sucking and pumping her vagina. Tracie put two fingers in her and that made Jody move her hips faster. Keeping in time with Tracie's finger, moving in and out of her. Finally, Jody took a hold of Tracie's shoulders and exploded with orgasm. She came so hard she felt like she was going to blackout from the intense pleasure. They were both spent. Jody had a feeling of relief inside her body and Tracie moved up to hold her.

"Do you want something to drink?" Tracie whispered.

"Yeah, but I don't want you to move. Let's just sleep," Jody said with a sleepy voice.

Tracie held her tightly and they both drifted off to slumber land.

The next morning, there was a persistent knocking on the door.

Tracie woke wondering who it could be. She eased out of bed, not wanting to disturb Jody. "Who is it?" she asked groggily.

"Mommy, it's me and Auntie Gail."

*Oh shit.* She opened the door. "This is a surprise, what are you two doing here?"

"When you didn't come home last night, I thought you'd be here, so we came to see if you want to go with us to breakfast."

"Please, Mommy, come with us," Sam excitedly said.

"How about if I meet your there? I gotta shower and get dressed. Gail, can I talk to you in the kitchen?"

"Sure," Gail said going to the kitchen.

"Jody's here so could you please take Sam to the restaurant and I'll see you in a few minutes?"

Gail stepped back with a smile on her face. "Does this mean you're back together?"

"I don't know but I'm hoping. Please go before she wakes up," Tracie said.

They walked back into the living room where Sam was sitting.

"You know, Sam your Mommy is right. She has to get ready, and we would probably be finished by the time she comes. I have a surprise for you! Let's call this Auntie Day and go to the movies.

"Yay," Sam said.

They gathered their things and headed off to breakfast. Tracie tried to ease the bedroom door open, but Jody was awake when she came in.

"Who was that? An old girlfriend?" Jody asked.

"No, just Sam and my sister Gail," Tracie said getting back into bed. "They came by to say hi. Gail's taking her to breakfast and the movie. How about breakfast? I can cook us something here or call for delivery if you're hungry."

"Thanks, but I have to go." Jody started to get out of bed.

"Why, why do you have to leave?"

"So much is happening, and I need time," Jody said dressing.

Tracie desperately wanted to argue but she sensed she'd better let her go. She didn't want to press her, not now, not when she felt Jody was close to remembering "When can I see you again?"

"Trace, after last night, I realized that we definitely were more than just friends."

"I hope you start to realize even more," Tracie said, following Jody out the bedroom door. She hoped for so much more.

Tracie didn't call for a few days, giving Jody time. Then one day she was walking alone in the park and saw a gay couple that looked so much in love. They reminded her of the love she and Jody had.

The thought of Jody made her realize that it was time to call. Thankfully, Jody agreed to see her. They saw each other every day but without Sam. They both felt it would be too hard on Sam if things

didn't work out. Jody was inhaling all the information Tracie could give out, trying to connect one person or event to another. She was still on leave from work, so Tracie picked her up and took her on adventures to different places. They talked to different people, did different things, trying to wiggle something free in her memory. Sometimes it worked and sometimes it didn't. Tracie made Jody see how important her therapy sessions were. Jody started going back to see Dr. Stable, sometimes Tracie and Ms. Jones went with her. They were all happy that things were finally settling down.

# Another Accident

Tracie's cell phone rang. It was Gail.

"There's been an accident," she blurted out. "It's Sam. She's at Cornell Medical." She said in between tears.

Tracie yanked her coat off the hook and ran to the nearest school exit. "What happened? Is she okay?" She ran to her car in the parking lot with her cell phone in hand, feeling like she was in another bad dream.

"I don't know," Gail said in between sobs. "Her school called me when they couldn't reach you.

Hurry, Tracie. I'll meet you there."

Tracie hung up from Gail and tried to call Jody but got no answer at her house. She was flooring the gas pedal to get to her baby.

When she entered the hospital, Sam's teacher was there.

"Please don't panic. She'll be okay. We were playing volleyball in the gym. She jumped for a ball and fell on her wrist. The doctor says it's sprained. They're bandaging her up now."

"Where is she?"

He pointed Tracie to a room two doors down. Tracie found Sam laying on a bed with her arm wrapped in a sling. The doctor was just finishing up.

"I'm her mother, Ms. Davis."

"Come in Ms. Davis we are almostt finished here except I have a prescription to give you in case she has too much pain.

"Thank you, Doctor." Tracie went to Sam and kissed her forehead.

"I want mommy Jody," Sam whined.

"Okay. I'll call her."

Just as Tracie went to call Ms. Jones's house for Jody, she saw Gail running through the door.

"How is she?" Gail asked frantically.

"She has a sprained wrist. She fell while playing volleyball. I'm calling Jody. Sam wants to see her."

"I'll go in and sit with her while you do that." Gail said

She dialed Ms. Jones' house and as soon as someone answered she blurted out. "Sam's in the hospital."

"What!" Ms. Jones said with disbelief.

"Sam's in the hospital. There was an accident. Where's Jody?"

Ms. Jones spoke to her in a rush. "What hospital? I'm on my way."

"Cornell, Where's Jody?" The phone clicked off without an answer.

Within thirty minutes, Ms. Jones was at the hospital.

Tracie saw Ms. Jones coming through the door. They met at the nurse's desk. "Where's Jody?" Tracie asked again. "Sam wants to see her."

Again Ms. Jones didn't answer her question concerning Jody. "What happened, Tracie?

What is the doctor saying?"

"She sprained her wrist."

Tracie explained everything the doctor had told her. "Why aren't you telling me where Jody is?"

Ms. Jones glanced away and said softly, "She's with Shawn."

This was too much. Her knees trembled. Their daughter needed her, and she's out with that fucking guy.

"What's she doing with him?" She wondered if she could really handle the answer. It was all too much.

"I don't know what's going on. All I know is he came by this afternoon and she left with him," Ms. Jones said.

Tracie just needed to be alone. "Okay," was all she could muster to say. Her priority

right now, was Sam. She'd deal with Jody later.

After seeing Sam, Ms. Jones said. "I called the house to see if she was back."

"Did you tell her about Sam?" Tracie asked wondering what Jody said.

"I just said there was an accident with Sam, and we were at Cornell hospital. She should take a cab here."

The pharmacy called letting them know Sam's prescription was ready. Tracie went to get it but had to wait because of the line in front of her. When she finally got back there was Jody in with Sam.

"Mommy Tracie look, mommy Jody is here.

"I see her. Jody can I speak to you for a minute."

"Where have you been? I called a couple of times when I first heard about Sam but got no answer." Tracie said it a little rougher than she meant to.

There was a pause and then Jody confessed. "Trace, I was with Shawn. I'm sorry. He came by today and said he was sorry for all that had happened. He said he wanted to take me to lunch to show there were no hard feelings. What he really wanted was to go over the same old bullshit. I should have been there for you and Sam. I just felt guilty about what I did to him. I thought he and I could be friends. That will never happen. I know that now."

"Let's go." Tracie said still mad that she wasn't there for Sam.

Sam was discharged. Ms. Jones walked with Jody who carried Sam. They walked to Tracie's car. Tracie and Gail walked ahead of them.

Gail had a big smile on her face. "It's really over with Richard this time. I don't know what happened, but my lawyer said the Judge let the pre-nup stand as is with no changes. He awarded me everything in the pre-nup. I guess he was tired of Richard and his lawyer. "I'm so happy for you, Gail. I think you need to get a dog it's time for us to go home." Tracie said looking back at Sam with her mother and grandmother.

# Christmas

Sam's wrist was healing. Their family was back to normal, as if the last months of heartache and heartbreak had never happened. Tracie realized everyday what a blessing it was to love and be loved.

"Any regrets?" Tracie asked Jody on Christmas day after a passionate love-making session.

"Yes, I regret what we had to go through. I sometimes wonder what would have happened if mom hadn't had that talk with me about Shawn. I wonder if I would have married him."

Tracie pulled her close. "I think you would have been miserable, like you were missing something in your life."

"Oh, and what would that have been?" Jody asked.

"Me, of course," Tracie said. "Who else can make you feel this way?"

Jody snuggled a little closer "Yeah baby, you're right about that."

Tracie was about to close her lips on one of Jody's breast when she heard a knock at the door and the telephone rang. Jody answered the telephone while Tracie started to get up for the door.

"Just a minute, Sam. I'll be out in a few. You can watch your cartoons while I get up," Tracie stood waiting to hear who was on the phone.

"That was Karen she wanted to let me know that the case against Sandy was dropped. The girl recanted everything."

"Who's Sandy?" Tracie asked

"Get back here." Jody said laying down propping up her head with her hand.

Tracie got back into to bed. Jody quickly Tracie about the case and that she'd represent Sandy if she still wanted to pursue her custody case.

"Mommy, Mommy hurry up," Sam said turning the knob of the locked door.

"Okay, Sweetie," Tracie said as she began to nibble on Jody's left breast. Jody moaned under her soft bites.

"Mommy, I want to open my presents and I'm hungry. I want some eggs and pancakes and syrup," Sam said through the door.

Jody managed a feeble response. "If you go count to twenty-five, Mommy Tracie will come out and make breakfast and we'll open presents while she cooks."

"Yay!" said Sam.

"Oh, thanks," Tracie whispered as she searched under the covers for Jody's wetness.

"That's okay," Jody whispered back.

They heard Sam running from the door and cartoons coming from the living room. Tracie found Jody's opening and entered her with two fingers.

Jody tensed as she felt Tracie coming into her and immediately relaxed her vaginal muscles. The rhythm of Tracie moving in and out of her took her to new heights of pleasure. She held onto Tracie's shoulders as she moved her hips in rhythm with her.

"Mommy, it's time," Sam said, interrupting their love making.

"Okay, we're coming." Tracie said

The three of them opened presents from under the tree then Tracie made breakfast. They made Christmas brunch right after breakfast while Sam played with her toys. Gail and Ms Jones came over at noon to eat and open more gifts with them. Jody's complete memory hadn't come back but enough was back that she knew that this was where she belonged.

Books From The Author

Aninoids – Young Adult sci-fi

A Stubborn Dog:GG – Adult true story

Ladies Love Advice – Adult

Man/Woman and A Murderer – Adult trans mystery (coming soon)

A Stubborn Dog:GG plus Mason Book 2 – Adult true story (coming soon)

# Don't miss out!

Visit the website below and you can sign up to receive emails whenever Anita Powell publishes a new book. There's no charge and no obligation.

https://books2read.com/r/B-A-RPAM-SYITB

Connecting independent readers to independent writers.

www.ingramcontent.com/pod-product-compliance
Lightning Source LLC
Chambersburg PA
CBHW021424150726
47989CB00001B/101